Communication Models

Uma Narula

ATLANTIC
PUBLISHERS & DISTRIBUTORS (P) LTD

Published by

ATLANTIC
PUBLISHERS & DISTRIBUTORS (P) LTD

B-2, Vishal Enclave, Opp. Rajouri Garden,
New Delhi-110027
Phones : 25413460, 25429987, 25466842

Sales Office
7/22, Ansari Road, Darya Ganj,
New Delhi-110002
Phones : 23273880, 23275880, 23280451
Fax : 91-11-23285873
web : www.atlanticbooks.com
e-mail : info@atlanticbooks.com

Printed in India
at Syndicate Binders, A-20, Hosiery Complex, Phase-II Extn., Noida

Dedicated to

Evolving Communication Models
In Communication decades

For
My family and Friends
Who
Go through process of Communication

Preface

The compilation of basic communication models is based on the evolution of communication models as developed by communication exemplars over a period of time in consequence to our changing understanding of the concepts, elements of communication process, and communication rules. Other models vis-à-vis Development Communication Models, International Communication and Globalization Models, Intercultural Models, Technology Models, Communication Management Models, Communication Research Models, Business Communication Models and Models for Communication Strategies and Planning are the product of my four decades of Communication research in theory and practice and publishing widely in the areas of development, culture and information technology.

The style of presenting communication concepts and strategies, concerns and challenges, from different perspectives in the framework of national and international framework in the form of models further enhances its value for it facilitates quick understanding.

Introduction focuses on Communication Framework, Concept of Communication and necessity for Communication Perspective. The book presents Communication Models in nine sections highlighting the perspectives from which human communications are practiced, interpreted and analyzed overtime.

The book would prove a useful aid in presenting communication in different perspectives to the students, teachers and trainers, researchers, practitioners, professionals, and educators who deal in diverse areas of Communications and focus on the critical issues pertaining to them. The book is cohesive and easily comprehensible.

Uma Narula

Contents

List of Figures and Tables

Pages

Introduction

Communication Framework

Over the last six decades there has been increasing interest in the study, applications, practice and research in Communication discipline. Research in Communication has conceptualized communication *per se* in 40s and 50s, and to develop Model and Theories. In short, to learn what communication is, how it works, and to develop means of communicating more effectively in diverse areas affecting human conditions in societal and economic contexts.

Earlier, Communication discipline had borrowed concepts and models from other disciplines of psychology, sociology, and anthropology etc. Over a period of time, it developed its own concepts, models, theories and assumptions through Communication Research. Such research has supported, refuted or improved upon various assumptions, constructs and other factors that have impact on changing perspectives on communication models, theories and practice. Various factors such as the historical analysis of communication theories, assessment of ongoing socio-economic and political realities, new insights and experiences gained through empirical research has created diverse communication perspectives. Moreover, human communication itself undergoing change due to various factors has impacted these perspectives.

Looking at communication as an essentially organizing feature of human society, over a period of time, different scholars with different assumptions and methods developed different paradigms to assess and evaluate the human communication *per se*.

Over a period of time different Mass Communication

Models developed in consequence to our changing understanding of the concepts, elements of communication process, and communication rules.

Researches also advocated, supported and developed different perspectives from which communication has been studied and applied overtime.

Change is an ongoing process in the human communication environment, in societal set-up and in information and communication technologies (ICT), and also in the development efforts by the societies. Such changes in these areas create new prospects for communication *per se*, for communication environment, and changes in conceptualizations both in theory and practice to meet the ever-changing demands.

The major constraint of these ever-changing demands is that communication is getting complex overtime. There are complexities in communication opportunities both technologically as well through social access. To coordinate communication complexities and the demands of the masses, newer rules and regulations, censorship and controls are created to restrain the opportunities. Another constraint is that, on one hand, the efforts to practice and create a globalization perspective on communication have made communication complex. On the other hand, it has created demands for culture specific models and communication perspectives since there is realization that every society has its own cultural identity, communication environment, role, rules and strategies.

But these two constraints have rather stimulated more theory and research and diverse perspectives in Communication discipline.

Concept of Communication

Communication is interaction with ourselves, with others and with our external and internal environments. The focus of our communication is sometimes defined, sometimes undefined and vague. Similarly not all times we are conscious of our purpose of communication or the effects that our messages will have on the targeted receivers. Our communication may not be comprehensible all time and for everyone. But communicate we must and we must express ourselves. It is necessary and important human activity to survive and grow.

The animals, the birds, the insects, the tree and the plants all communicate. To us it may not be comprehensible just as our communication may not be comprehensible to them.

Human communication and non-human communication through technology is the context of our discussions.

The human effort is to discover nature, essence, and dynamics of communication to learn what communication is and how it works and to develop means of communicating more effectively. Over the last few decades, there has been increasing interest in the study and practice of 'communication'. As a result, knowledge and definition of 'communication' has varied widely in terms of purpose, nature, level of abstraction and scope.

In human (public) communication, three major elements play a significant role. These are Ethos, Logos, and Pathos. Ethos refers to the character of the speaker, Logos is power of reason and evidenced in text and speech and Pathos is emotions elicited in an audience.

Communication is a social process, and countless ways in which human beings keep in touch with one another. The messages in a shared environment could not only be oral, written, non-verbal, visual or olfactory but these could also be laws, customs, practices, ways of dressing, gestures, buildings, flags, gardens, exhibits, etc. Language and body synthesizers that are culture specific are essential components of messages. People in communication define the various types of society, sub-society and groups. The characteristics of these depend on the modes of communication they possess, media exposure, rituals and personal relationships.

The conventional concept of communication is that we use communication to express our inner purposes, attitudes, and feelings; to describe events and objects of the external world and to produce sharing between the speaker and the audience addressed. The patterns of social communication constitute the world, as we know it.

Pearce (1989) presents the premise that we live in communication rather than outside of communication and use communication for our own purposes. In the era of communication revolution, communication is far more important and central to human condition than ever before realized. There is recognition that multiple forms of communication exist in human society. These forms are not neutral. They are alternative forms of being human. Each qualitatively different form of communication affords a particular array of opportunities and problems.

Communication is the locus of forces through which persons create and manage social realities. Social reality includes concept of Self, Community, Institutions, and Cultures. Through communication we create concept of SELF–who we are, we create relationships within the community and build institutions. We communicate and act together to create and recreate community relationships that are managed within a culture.

Communication has been subjected to numerous and diverse conceptualizations. However, most definitions agree that:

- Human communication is a process of transmission of ideas through feelings and behavior from one person to another.
- Communication is persuasive and seeks to obtain desirable response to what is being transmitted.
- Communication is not linear but is a two-way and multi-way process.

Modes of Communication have evolved overtime, from oral traditions to electronics and wireless. They have expanded from local to regional, national and global, thus crossing all the physical barriers. There are three main divisions of communication modes: Non-verbal communication is thorough silence, gestures, tactile, olfactory and space-time cues. Verbal communication comprising of spoken word is through both interpersonal and electronic channels. Written communication is through Print media, electronic media and wireless and online channels.

Three types of channels are used for the above three modes of communication: Interpersonal, Non-verbal, and Mass Media both electronic and wireless.

In interpersonal, there can be one on one, and small group communication like in group meetings, seminars and teaching classes. Both verbal and non-verbal channels are used. Sometimes in group meetings supportive written communication may be used such as flip charts, posters and brochures etc. In impersonal interpersonal mode the mass audience is the communication focus such as audience in political rallies. Body language, space and time cues are important when non-verbal cues are used in interpersonal communication. Thus the oral traditions of interpersonal through various modes and the oral traditions that we label now as traditional media or popular media are the folklores and performing arts. These are the earliest forms of human communications through ages.

The earliest communication scenario thought of communication as linear activity. This was a simplistic presentation of human communication. Sender sends the message through a channel to the receiver. But an interaction and processural perspective of communication evolved through research in theory and practice.

It evolved that communication activity is a process. The essential elements are: there is interaction so there is sender/s and receiver/s within a context. There is a message to be conveyed through a channel. The objective of the interaction is to have intended or unintended effects on receivers (targeted audience), to assess the effectiveness, their should be loops of feedback between the sender and receiver.

In the process of transmission, certain distortions get added which are not part of the message sent by the source. This they called NOISE. There is *Channel noise* that suggests interference with the transmission of the message. Channel noise has various connotations. In media channels, it could be identified with the state of technology, operation of technology, physical (through purchasing power), and social access to these channels; and people's actual exposure to these messages. In interpersonal communication, channel noise may be any distraction or distortion of message between the source and the receiver.

Semantic Noise occurs when message is misunderstood because of lack of understanding of communicator's frame of reference. The receiver does not ascribe the same meaning to the message as intended by the communicator. Or the receiver does not understand the message because the communicator may use difficult words and unknown terminology.

In case the sender is not satisfied with the passive reception of the message irrespective of such passivity from mass media or interpersonal channels. He/she wants more control on communication — i.e. whether the message has the intended effect or not. The concept of linear feedback is added. Further control can be achieved if the sender knows receivers' reactions to the messages. Thus it is necessary for the receiver to give feedback to the sender and certain cues about the message. This helps the sender to maintain control over the intended effects and adjust future messages.

The need for communication channels, messages and audience for the focused issues varied and these developed accordingly over the time periods. The communication policies related to these issues are formed to organize the communication scenario effectively.

Taking a Communication Perspective

The propensity to differentiate Communication from NOT Communication follows one of Aristotle's laws of identity. In contemporary thought, Aristotelian heritage is expressed in the assumption that one communicates not only by speaking, reading and writing but also by sleeping, eating, running, etc. There is little difficulty in identifying a particular instance of social action as *Communication*. The problem arises in specifying what human actions are *not communications*. It is impossible to identify a set of "critical attributes" to differentiate between what is communication and what is not communication. Any form of social action can be shown to be communication.

Narula & Pearce (1986) argue that communication is better understood as a perspective or context from which any act may be examined or understood. The assumption is that any action has a message value. One cannot, *NOT COMMUNICATE*. Whatever one does or does not do can be looked at from a communication perspective.

From a communication perspective, the human actions are seen as the process by which people collectively maintain social realities. Human beings simultaneously live in a symbolic universe (social reality) and are engaged in sequences of interactions with their environments and with other people. They actively strive to create coherent stories drawing from the "resources" of their social reality and from the practices in which they are engaged with others.

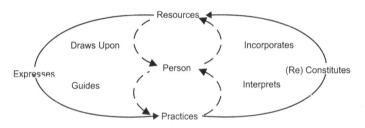

Fig. 1. Communication Perspective

Implications are that the 'communication perspective' facilitates interpretative and critical analysis. The result of this analysis is that meanings of actions, both of one's own and that of others, are made transparent and increase the possibility of communication. Thus from the point of theory, research and practice, communication - whether inter-personal or mass media always has a context in which it is presented, received, reacted to and acted upon. The contexts could be cultural, development, international, and technological. Thus utilization or effectiveness of communication is placed in contexts and is therefore context specific.

In these specific contexts we present eight perspectives from which human communications is practiced, interpreted and analyzed. These are Basic Communications, Development Communications, Information Communication Technology (ICT), International Communication and Globalization, Intercultural Communication, Communication Management, Business Communication Practices and Communication Research. These perspectives do overlap and all these perspectives are intertwined as *a Communication Perspective.*

From these perspectives, many social actions that otherwise would not be defined as instances of communication, are shown to be powerful means of creating and managing social reality. For example, consider public works and legislation; from a communication perspective, both powerfully construct the social realities of the masses and the government itself.

Social constructionist perspective on communication treats actions as real, pivotal events rather than simply as transitory states of or between pre-existing entities. That is, the events and objects of the social world exist because of patterns of actions that have accrued previously, and actions are being performed now to bring them into being. Secondly, social constructionists think of communication in terms of interactive patterns and not atomistic units.

Communication planning through interactive patterns is an integral part of a holistic communication perspective. Communication planning is necessary to make varied perspectives action oriented. Communication planning involves, communication strategies, media planning (channel planning) and resource management culminating in communication policies.

COMMUNICATION MODELS

A MODEL is presentation of the real phenomenon in abstract terms that can be applied in different forms at different times. Communication is an extremely complex process that becomes more complex with ever-changing communication phenomenon. Complexity and constant change in communication process makes it imperative that it is presented in simple and generalized way to explain and understand the structure and functions of communications. Communication Models present this simplification.

1

Basic Communication Models

Classification of Communication Models

The format of communication models depends on how we define and understand the process of communications and how these are applicable to different forms of communications. Communication Models are classified in three categories: stages, types, and forms of models. There have been four stages in the development of Communication Models: *Action, Interaction, Transaction and Convergence.* There are two types of communication models: *Linear and Non-Linear.* These can be presented in various forms such as *Symbolic Model, Physical Models, Mental Models, Verbal Models, Iconic Models, Analog Models and Mathematical Models.*

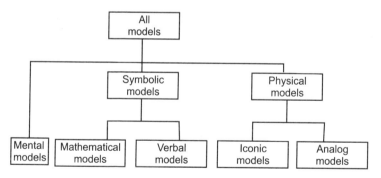

Fig. 1.1. Types of Communication Models

This presents taxonomy of models. In communication we are concerned with Symbolic models that comprise of Verbal models and Mathematical models. Physical models comprises of Iconic and Analog models. Verbal model is simply the theory stated in words. Verbal models are useful in terms of stating hypothesis or presenting results of a study. Verbal models could be SMCR models of communication process, SMCRE model of David Berlo and Gerbner's general model of communication.

Graphic models present schematically what verbal models present with words. Graphic models of communications are: Gerbner's general Model of communications, Westley and Mclean's ABC mass communication Model, Defleurs expansion of Shannon and Weavers Model and Vora's Model for diffusing concepts. These models are discussed in later section.

Iconic models are photographs, sculptures, and paintings of person, objects and scenes. Analog models bear a defined structural relationship to the subject they represent but do not look like them. The computer may be described as an analog of the human brain.

Mathematical models are not frequently encountered in communication field except for graph theory in the analysis of communication networks and the statistical concepts of information processing. Communication theories generally have not been expressed in mathematical symbols.

Communication system comprises of two general models: Media systems and Oral systems. In media systems, the information flow is activated through professional communicators for transmission through media channels such as print, radio, television, film, video, telecommunications etc. The messages are descriptive and impersonal. In the oral systems, the messages are point to point emanated from sources authorized to speak by social hierarchy. Messages are prescriptive and they are transmitted through oral channels to highly differentiated audience. Each primary group completes the diffusion pattern by acting as a relay channel of communication within and between groups. Interpersonal channels can be personal when the communication is between or among the individuals. The direction of change is from oral to media systems in all societies. But at the same time they coexist and are supportive of each other.

Linear and Non-linear Models of Communications. This is

second classification of models. The media system and oral system models are classified into Linear and Non-linear Communication Models.

Linear Model is unidirectional model that portrays the message flow from speaker to audience with or without effect. These models could be both vertical and horizontal. In Non-linear models the message flow is bi-directional or multidirectional. These models are circular and convergence models.

Most of the earlier models of communication in 40s and 50s were linear models. They are foundation models and suggested new, useful and significant concepts, which were later, developed into non-linear, interaction, transaction and convergence models.

The linear communication models were useful for, and designed for experiments that assumed one-way causality for the study of propaganda and mass persuasion. These models described a simple communication act and not the process. Although Berlo in 60s defined communication in terms of communication process but in his subsequent research he did not pursue this idea. In fact Berlo (1977) acknowledged that S-M-C-R was not intended as a communication model but it was developed as an audio-visual aid to develop recall of the components of the communication relationships.

There are limitations of the linear models. Kincaid (1979) pointed seven biases of linear models for human communications:

- The linear models give a one-way-act usually vertical, and not cyclical-two-way process overtime.
- A source biased based dependency rather than on the relationship of those who communicate and interdependency.
- A tendency to focus on the objects of communication as if they existed in vacuum, and isolated from their context.
- A tendency to focus on the messages *per se* at the expense of silence, punctuation, and timings of the messages.

- A tendency to consider the primary function of communication to be persuasion rather than mutual understanding, agreement and collective action.

- A tendency to concentrate on psychological effects of communication on separate individuals rather than the social effects and relationships among the individuals.

- A belief in one-way mechanistic causation rather than mutual causation, which characterize human information systems that are fundamentally cybernetic.

Freire (1973) suggested that these seven biases are interrelated and cumulative, each tend to support the other and tend to create a coherent image of the communication process in spite of the limitations and problems it produces.

The *Non-linear Models* follow the cybernetic principle. The four most important elements of cybernetic explanation are the concept of information, feedback, networks and purpose. The analytical concepts of interaction, self-generation, mutual exchange and sharing explain the human communication in non-linear models of communication.

Deutch Karl (1968, p. 390) advocated that human systems are not connected and coordinated by mechanical means or force of matter and energy but rather by exchange of information. The most important for information sharing is the communication network circuits, by which individuals within the system are interconnected. A circuit is a circular loop with two-way exchange of information that is a prerequisite for feedback. Feedback produces action in response to input of information and through its reactions modify its subsequent behavior.

Capra (1975, pp. 286, 296) suggests a '*Bootstrap Model*'. It suggests that process of communication is self-generating by mutual sharing and exchange of information. According to this model, the universe is a dynamic web of interrelated events. Mutual interrelation determines the structure of the web. None of the property of any part of the web is fundamental. They all follow from overall consistency.

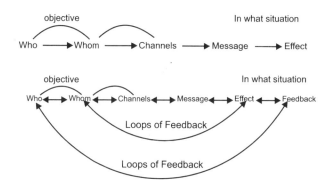

Fig. 1.2. Linear and Non-linear Models of Communication

The third classification of communications model is: Action Model, Interaction Model, Transaction Model and Convergence Model. Action, interaction, transaction and convergence concepts developed these types of communication Models. They were rather the developmental stages of communication models.

The Action Models are sender-oriented. They emphasize how a sender must construct a message to secure a desired result. How must the sender act, or speak in order to transmit his message and persuade his listeners.

Action models may work with media channels but they do not work well with interpersonal channels. From the action model point, the miscommunication may come from two perspectives. One, the source did not structure the message correctly for transmission. Two, the listeners did not correctly listen to the message or the listeners applied their own meaning to the message.

The action model is implicit model for both listening as well speaking. Listening is the act of receiving the message, and it is acting upon the message. People who operate from action model presume that listening just happens and it does not require the active participation of the people. Listening skills need not be developed and people are natural effective listeners. To them, listening is unrelated to the source. These misassumptions make the mass mediated messages ineffective at times. The early models (1.3 to 1.8) were action models.

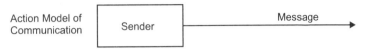

Fig. 1.3. Action Model of Communication

Interaction Models focused on interaction and relatedness between the sender and receiver. The concern was the effect of the message on both senders and receivers. The communication theorists and researchers were not satisfied with the passive reception of the message. They wanted more control on communication i.e. whether the message has the intended effect or not. They added the concept of linear feedback. Further, control can be achieved if the sender knows receivers' reactions to the messages. Thus it is necessary for the receiver to give feedback to the sender and certain cues about the message. This helps the sender to maintain control over the intended effects and adjust future messages accordingly.

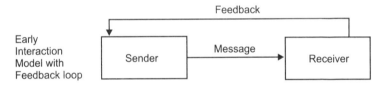

Fig. 1.4. Interaction Model of Communication

When the dimension of 'time' was added in the model, the linear qualities of the model became more apparent. It is apparent from Fig. 1.4. that the exchange of message is taking place overtime. The sender is alternatively sending a message and receiving feedback from the receiver. There is continuity of responses between the sender and the receiver. Sender has control over the intended effect of the message and adjusts future messages as desired by the sender to be effective message.

In an interaction model, *listening* becomes a process of listening, receiving, decoding, interpreting and acting upon messages. When the receiver acts upon the message; that behavior is seen as *feedback* and is seen as *response* to the sender's message.

Mother tells the child, 'Tara, please clean your book bag'.

She comes after a few minutes and finds Tara cleaning the study desk including the book bag. Since the message did not have the desired behavior on child's part, mother gave another message, 'hey I only wanted you to clean your book bag'.

There was interaction listening between mother and Tara. People who listen interactionally are not essentially good listeners. They are so preoccupied with how they are going to respond to the message that they do not receive the message as intended or distort the message received. As an alternative, if Tara had given the feedback that she would like to clean the study table along with the book bag, then mother could have adjusted her second message accordingly.

The concept of information is a significant contribution in interaction approach to communication. What is *new* is informational, what is not *new* is redundancy. In communication, the relationship between information and redundancy is meaningful. Wherever there is redundancy, there is repetition of elements forming a pattern. These patterns and differences in patterns are meaningful within interaction. They are *patterns of interaction*. In communication, patterns of interaction and variations are more meaningful than the information itself.

Although information is an important concept in communication theory, but we tend to base our behavior more on variations in pattern of interactions than on the amount of information in our communications. Communications may be personal or mass mediated.

There are two limitations of Interaction Models. One, the true interaction is lacking between the sender and the receiver. Separate behaviors (action and responses) are exchanged in interaction models that alternate in sending and receiving messages. Second, interaction models lose their clarity when they are applied to the multiple message systems operating simultaneously.

Transactional Models of Communication view communication as simultaneous responses whereas linear feedback is central in the interaction models. In transaction models, while 'A' is speaking, 'B' is generating messages or feedback in many ways ... through body postures, facial expressions, eye movements, hand gestures, spatial distance from 'A' and verbal language use.

If we attempt to diagram the flow of these messages and potential messages generated by both A&B through their specific message systems; the overlapping lines begin to merge into simultaneous interactions. That is the characteristic of transactional model.

Fig. 1.5. Transactional Model of Communication

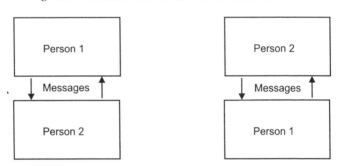

Fig. 1.5. Transactional Model of Communication

In Interaction model 'A' may be interacting with 'B' and there may be linear feedback. But in Transaction Model both A&B are participating simultaneously in the communication situation. They mutually perceive each other. Both, sender and the receiver are making adjustments to the messages exchanged within transactions. Thus both the parties are engaged in the process of creating meaning in a relationship.

In the Transaction Model, we observe the entire communication situation rather than isolating a sender or a receiver. Because we view the entire transaction, we view the progress of communication by re-examining the transaction at a later time.

In transactional models, the concern is with the *patterns of communication behavior* within the relationship formed between the senders and the receivers; and not with *patterns of information and redundancy*. Communication can be effective by making use of these identified patterns of communication behavior. It is not necessary to know what causes such behavior patterns, what motivates them or even how they are created. As long as a pattern of behavior can be defined and observed, it can be used advantageously. Advertisers spend millions to discover patterns of product users' behavior.

Convergence Model of Communication is based on the principle of cybernetics. The four most important elements of cybernetic explanation are the concept of information, feedback, networks and purpose. The analytical concepts of interaction, self-generation, mutual exchange and information sharing and mutual understanding explain the human communication in convergence models. They are non-linear models of communication.

Kincaid (1979) developed a convergence model. According to this model, effective feedback creates convergence and ineffective feedback creates divergence. The participants converge and diverge on their relative positions overtime to reach mutual understanding of the issue. In this model *communication is reaching mutual understanding.*

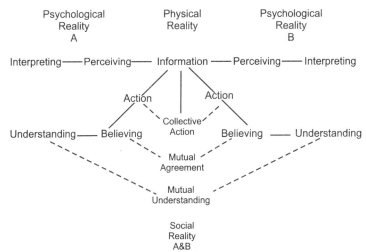

Fig. 1.6. Basic Components of Convergence Model of Communication

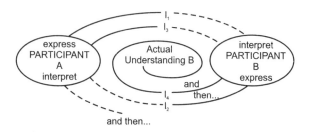

Fig. 1.7. Convergence Model of Communication

In the last six decades there has been a great model hunt for Communication Models. Empirical and Communication research influenced the evolution of these models.

The basic linear models of 40s and 50s are foundation models and suggested new, useful and significant concepts which were later developed and integrated into non-linear interaction, transaction and convergence models of 80s. These models developed the new concepts of multiple feedback loops for mutual understanding among the participants, and contextual approach in communication act and situation. Further, the emphasis has been in developing specific models rather than a Meta Communication Model. Specific models may be culture specific, system specific and situation specific.

Therefore, basic models Fig. 1.7 through Fig. 1.32 given in our text are essentially foundation models in communication discipline.

Table 1.8. Models of Communication: Summary (A)

Lasswell (1948)	Gerbner (1956)	Berlo (1960)
WHO Communicating organizations, their nature and function.	1. SOMEONE (Source, communicator) 2. perceives an event 3. and reacts 4. in a situation to make available	SOURCE Press, publishing research organizations, governments, churches and other social organizations, television, radio and publishing
says WHAT The nature of the content: informative entertaining, educative. in which	6. MATERIALS 7. in some form 8. and context 9. conveying content through some	MESSAGE Words, mathematical symbols, pictorial images
CHANNEL Print media, audiovisual media automatic data processing.	5. MEANS channels; media; physical engineering administrative and institutional facilities for distribution and control.	CHANNEL Print, electronic media
to WHOM The nature and receptivity of the audience.	1. SOMEONE (destination, audience) 2. perceives an event 3. and reacts 4. in a situation	RECEIVER General audiences, specialized audiences
and with what	of some	
EFFECT The nature and effect or response of the audience; the way in which it *affects* the communicator.	10. CONSEQUENCE Someone perceives an event and reacts in a situation through some means to make available materials in some form and context conveying content of some on sequence to.	

Table 1.9. Models of Communication: Summary (B)

	Sources	Type of Model	Main Components of the Model	Definitions of Communication
1.	Claude Shannon and and Warren Weaver (1949)	Linear	source encoder message decoder destination noise feedback	All the procedures by which one mind may affect another.
2.	Charles Osgood and others (1957)	Linear	message decoder interpreter encoder message decoder	One system a source, influences another, the destination by manipulation of alternative signals which can be transmitted over the channel connecting them.
3.	Bruce Westley and Malcolm MacLean (1957), based on Newcomb (1953)	Linear	messages sources (advocacy roles) gatekeepers (channel roles receivers (behavioural system roles) feedback	Person A transmit message about an object X to person B through gatekeeper C.
4.	David Berlo (1960)	Linear	source message channel receiver feedback	A process by which a source intentionally changes the behaviour of a receiver.
5.	Wilbur Schramm (1973)	Relational	informational signs relationship among participants active receivers	A set of communication acts focussed on a set of informational signs within a particular relationship.
6.	D. Lawrence Kincaid (1979)	Conver- gence	informtion uncertainty convergence mutual understanding mutual agreement collective action networks of relationships	A process of convergence in which information is shared by participants in order to reach a mutual understanding.

Functions of Communication Models

Communication Models are visualization of the communication process. They are basics about the elements of communication, how they operate and interact.

Models may serve any or all of the four general functions. First, models organize the various elements and the process of the communication act in a meaningful and interesting way. Second, they help in discovery of new facts about communication. It generates research questions. It serves heuristic function. Third, these enable us to make predictions concerning communications i.e. what will happen under certain conditions. Fourth, models may provide the means of measuring the elements and processes involved in communication.

Frank E.X. Dance (1983) suggested that we adopt a family of communication models. Each of these models highlights some aspect of the process of communication and distorts others. Most communication theorists agreed. After 1970, few more models of communication were developed and those models of communication were not unidirectional. For detailed discussion on evolution of Models of Communication, refer to Narula (1994, pp. 45-69).

The various Communication Models that developed in the last six decades reflect on the process of communication. The revised concept of communication is based on empirical communication research and deliberations of scholars in the discipline. Key points of these revised models are:

- Communication is processural and reflexive
- Sequence of events is important
- Meaning of events is derived from their locations within an ongoing sequence
- We learn to focus on "patterns" rather than on individual messages, and on interactions rather than on movements of messages from one place to another
- Participants in the communication process contribute to the meaning of any given aspect of communication and function as 'sources' and 'receivers' as they participate.

- There is interaction between the sender and receiver through several communication networks and feedback loops.

- Contextual approach to meaning in a communication act and situation is important and mutual understanding among the participants is necessary for effective communication.

The essential elements of the process are presented in the following five versions of the Basic Communication Model:

1. Sender—message——channel——receiver

2. Sender—message——channel

3. Sender—message——channel——receiver——effects

4. Sender—message——channel——receiver——effects——feedback

5. Sender—message——channel——receiver——effects——feedback loops

Fig. 1.10. Basic Communication Model-1

In version 1 of the Basic Model, the objective of the sender is to send message through a channel to the targeted receiver. The sender's immediate concern is not receivers' reactions, comprehensibility, and intended effects e.g. communication through public meetings or presentation on TV. Here the receivers are not differentiated mass and there could be both short and long-term effect that the sender is not assessing. In version 2 of the Model, the targeted audience exists but it is their choice to attend the public meeting or switch on the TV.

In version 3 of the Model, the targeted receivers are differentiated; sender is concerned about the intended effects of his/her message. He/she is vaguely aware of the effects; but he/she has no way to assess the effects. In version 4 of the Model, the targeted receivers are differentiated, sender is concerned about the intended and unintended effects of his/her message and he/she assesses the effects through audience feedback.

In version 5 of the Model, the targeted receivers are differentiated, sender is concerned about the intended and unintended effects of his/her message and he/she wants his/her audience to comprehend his/her message. In order to assess the effects on the audience and to facilitate comprehensibility of the message, feedback loops are necessary. Feedback loops from sender to receiver and from receiver to sender are necessary in these contexts. The receiver can choose a channel of his/her choice for feedback, which is equally accessible to him and the primary sender.

These basic Models for communications evolved overtime.

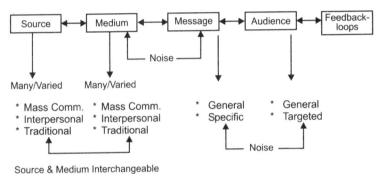

Fig. 1.11. Basic Communication Model-2

Aristotle's Model of Communication

Aristotle proposed the earliest communication model some 2300 years back. This is simple and linear. This model included five essential elements of communication: the speaker, the speech or message, the audience, the occasion and the effect. Aristotle advises the speaker on constructing a speech for different audience on different occasions and for different effects. This model is actually more applicable to public speaking than interpersonal communication.

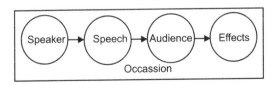

Fig. 1.12. Aristotle's Model of Communication

Lasswell Model of Communication

Lasswell proposed a communication model in 1948 that was not different from Aristotle. This model suggests the message flow in a pluralistic society with multiple audiences. The message flow is through numerous channels.

Communication Component	Research Area
Who	Control Analysis
Says What	Content Analysis
In What Channel	Media Analysis
To Whom	Audience Analysis
With What Effect	Effect Analysis

Table 1.13. Lasswell Model of Communication

Shannon and Weaver Model of Communication

In 1949, Claude Shannon and Warner Weaver proposed a Communication Model. The speaker selects a desired message from all the possible messages. The message is send through a communication channel and changed into signals (messages). The receiver receives the signals. In the process of transmission, certain distortions get added which are not part of the message sent by the source. This they called NOISE.

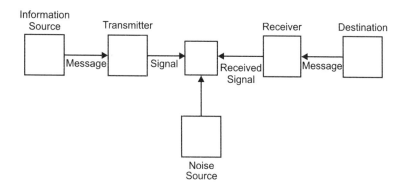

Fig. 1.14. Shannon and Weaver Model of Communication

This model led to the technical improvements in the message transmissions and it stimulated scholars from several disciplines to study communication scientifically. Their effort was towards developing a *Unified Model of Communication.* The focus of this Model was three components viz. Channel Noise, Semantic Noise, and Feedback. These three components were considered for the first time in the communication process. *Channel noise* suggested any interference with the transmission of the message. *Semantic Noise* occurs when message is misunderstood. *Feedback* is the third component to assess the 'effects' and comprehend the intended message adequately.

Narula (1994) discussing about 'Noise' i.e. distortions in communication transmission suggests that channel noise has various connotations. In media channels, it could be identified with the state of technology, operation of technology, physical (through purchasing power), and social access to these channels; and people's actual exposure to these messages. In interpersonal communication, channel noise may be any distraction or distortion of message between the source and the receiver.

Further, *Semantic Noise* occurs when message is misunderstood because of lack of understanding of communicator's frame of reference. The receiver does not ascribe the same meaning to the message as intended by the communicator. Or the receiver does not understand the message because the communicator may use difficult words and unknown terminology.

Fig. 1.15. Channel Noise

Communicator places his message in a selected channel to reach audience (A), but it is subject to noise interference.

Communicator and audience member (A) has same frame of reference so they understand the message, A1 is partially receptive, A2 is unable to understand.

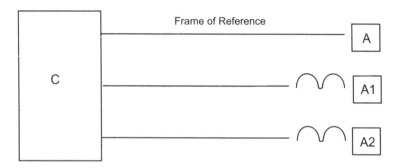

Fig. 1.16. Semantic Noise

Communicator in a channel controlled by 'E' reports source message. For instance, pro family planning messages of the government (source) is reported by professional communicators through opinion leaders to the villagers. Opinion leaders are second in line communicators to the people. The original source can pass messages through two-step communicators. Some can receive message directly if they have direct exposure to media channel, others indirectly through opinion leaders. Messages may not register at all with others who are inattentive to them.

Thus the feedback interactions occur along the communication route. But these feedback interactions are only one-way.

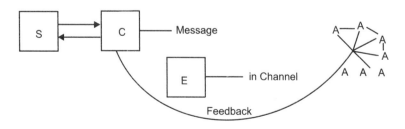

Fig. 1.17. Channel and Semantic Noise

Shannon and Weaver did discuss the semantic or pragmatic problem in communication and the channel noise in the transmission of messages. But their model failed since other human communication researchers who used this model did not consider enough about the semantic or pragmatic levels of communications. They did not pay enough attention to the channel noise. It did not register with them that feedback component is a significant component in communication process.

Principle of redundancy i.e. the repetition of the main idea of the message is used to reduce channel noise both in mass media and interpersonal communication channels. The semantic noise can be reduced if communicator adjusts his vocabulary to audience needs, interests and understanding. But the interpretation of intended meaning depends on feedback loops between the source and the receiver.

Wendell Johnsons Model of Communication

Wendell Johnsons proposed one of the most insightful models in 1951. It is a simple model explaining the complex process of communication.

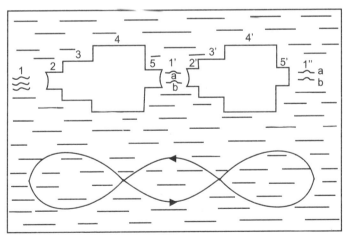

Fig. 1.18. Wendell Johnsons Model of Communication

In the figure, the surrounding rectangle indicates that communication takes place in a *context*. This context is external to both the sender and the receiver and even to the communication process as well. The curved loop indicates that the various stages of communications are actually interrelated and interdependent.

Stage 1 in the figure denotes communication event and the actual communication process begins at this point. This event is the external stimulus to communication. Although all communication may not have reference to this event. Johnsons argues that communication make sense when it relates to the external world. Stage 1' is the external event of spoken or written words that served stimulation for the speaker.

At stage 2, the receiver is stimulated through one or more sensory channels. The opening at 2 is shown relatively small to emphasize that out of a large number of sensory stimulations, only a small part stimulates the receiver. At stage 2' the receiver is stimulated

At stage 3, the organic evaluations occur. Certain bodily changes are affected such as muscular tensions. At stage 3' there are organism evaluations.

At stage 4, the feelings that are aroused at stage 3 are translated into words in accordance with individual's unique language habits. Stage 4' feelings of receiver are translated into words.

At stage 5, the selected linguistic symbols are arranged into a pattern. Stage 5' shows the selected linguistic pattern. These symbols serve as stimulation for another receiver.

This is a continuous process. This model is not a complete explanation of the communication process *per se*. It is rather an attempt to picture some of the most essential elements, processes and relevant relationships that make up the communication act.

The major contribution of this Model is the *Interaction* and *Contextual* components in the communication models that were developed later on.

Wilbur Schramm Model of Communication

Wilbur Schramm was influential in facilitating use of

linear models in 1950's and later on moved to develop relational models in 1973. Empirical and communication research influenced his models.

1. The Sender → Receiver model of early 40s based on bullet theory.

2. The Sender → Message → Receiver (as Schramm realized the importance of message)

3. Sender → message → channel → receiver. (On further research the importance of channel was evidenced).

   Sender → message → channel → receiver → effects.

Fig. 1.19. Wilbur Schramm Model of Communication

In his relational models of 70s Schramm was concerned with the effects of communication on the receivers. He used the *effects* and *effects analysis* components from Berlo's Model of 1960. He implicitly suggested *Interaction* component when he talked about active, selective and manipulative audience in his relational model. He argued that the most dramatic change in general communication theory in the last 40 years has been the abandonment of the idea of passive audience. Audience is a full partner in the process of communication.

David Berlo's Model of Communication (1960) explains the various components in the communication process. The four basic components are source, message, channel and receiver. There are five channels for each of these four components. It was for the first time that the '*Effect*' component was initiated in the communication process. Berlo suggested that message must have some effect positive or negative on the audience and that effect must be assessed through effect analysis.

Source →	Message →	Channel →	Receiver → Effects
Communication Skills	Elements	Seeing	Communication Skills
Attitudes	Structure	Hearing	Attitudes
Knowledge	Content	Touching	Knowledge
Social System	Treatment	Smelling	Social System
Culture	Code	Tasting	Culture

Fig. 1.20. Berlo's Model of Communication

Gerbner's Model of Communication

Gerbner's Model of Communication (1956) considers these elements in the communication process. There is source that reacts to an event in a situation through some channel. The content and the consequences of the communication act are conveyed in some form and context. This model emphasized the importance of *effects* and *context* in the communication process and act.

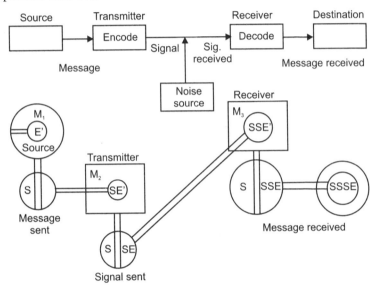

Fig. 1.21. Gerbner's Model of Communication 1

Communication Component	Research Area
Someone	Communicator/Audience Research
Perceives an Event	Perception Research and Theory
And Reacts	Effectiveness Measurement
In a Situation	Physical/Social Setting Research
Through Some Means	Media Investigation
To Make Available Materials	Administration; Distribution
In Some Form	Structure; Organization; Style
And Context	Communicative Setting
Conveying Content	Content Analysis; Study of Meaning
Of Some Consequence	Overall Changes Study

Table 1.22. Gerbner's Model of Communication 2

Westley and MacLean Model of Communication

Westley and MacLean's Model (1957) expanded on the Newcombs ABX model (A communicates to B on topic X) with the inclusion of C as gatekeeper as developed by Lewin. The A_s representing advocacy roles select and transmit messages purposely to modify B_s perception of X. The B_s (perceivers and audience members representing behavioral system roles) respond in terms of their needs and requirement for messages as means of orienting themselves to the environment. The C_s (representing channel roles or gatekeepers) are agents of the B_s who non-purposely select and transmit information for them.

Linear feedback is an important component of this model and introduced first time in the communication model.

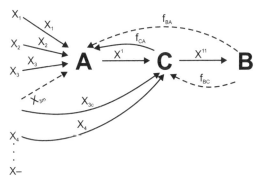

Fig. 1.23. Westley and MacLean Model of Communication

DeFleur Model of Mass Communication System

The DeFleur Model (1966) expanded on the Shannon and Beaver Model and interjected a mass medium device. Based on Westley and MacLean Model suggested feedback device to demonstrate that communication process is circular and thus implicitly suggested two-way feedback. The 'noise' in the model may interfere at any stage in the mass communication process. DeFleur pictures the source, transmitter, receiver and destination as separate phases of mass communication. The components of *two-way feedback and targeted audience* (as separate from receiver) were introduced first time in the Communication Model.

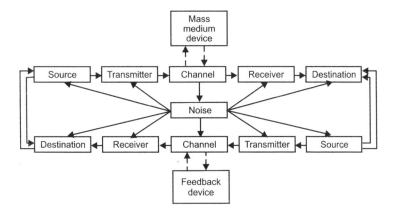

Fig. 1.24. DeFleur Model of Mass Communication System

Hiebert, Urgurait and Bohn (HUB) Model of Mass Communication

In this model, communication is perceived as a set of concentric circles much like the waves formed when a pebble is thrown in a pool. The pebble that is analogous to the communication content causes ripples that become ever widening circles until they hit the shore (audience) and bounce back (feedback).

The idea is that initial content goes through a series of actions and reactions labelled as pool of human affairs. The focus on content development was given attention for the first time.

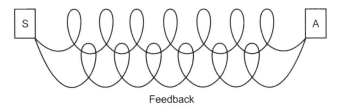

Feedback

Fig. 1.25. HUB Model of Mass Communication

Vora's Model for Diffusion of Concepts

Vora's model is a complex model. It presents the concept of diffusion, knowledge, attitude change, and behavior change in a dynamic and progressive spiral that utilizes mass media and interpersonal channels. This model emphasized the *external and internal environment and effects components* in addition to source, message, channel and receiver components in the mass communication process for diffusion of concepts.

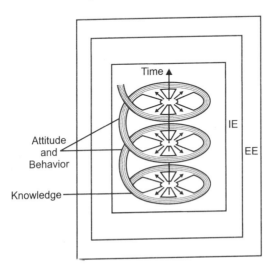

Fig. 1.26. Vora's Model for Diffusion Concepts

Effective Interpersonal Communication Model

Generally any good communication is labelled as effective if it reaches its targeted audience. Both mass media and interpersonal communication need to be effective to achieve its objectives.

Interpersonal communication describes the relationship between the 'Self and Others' and the coordination between the two. Effective interpersonal communication is characterized by five qualities of openness, empathy, being supportive and positive. Openness is willingness to reveal information about oneself that is relevant in the interpersonal encounter. Empathy is feeling as the other person feels and one identifies with the other. This helps in understanding the attitude and behavior of the other persons. Supportive environment facilitates the open and empathetic communication and it becomes effective. Person must have positive regard for oneself. Equally important is having positive feelings about the other persons. This encourages active and meaningful participation and interaction. Positive feelings of general communication situations are important for effective interaction.

Interpersonal Communication Models

Bois' Model of semantic reaction (1973) referred as 'Semantic Reactor's is most useful and insightful for interpersonal communication.

Fig. 1.27. Bois' Model of Semantic Reactor

The Self responds to stimuli as a whole, a reaction is determined by actual situation, spoken word, the thought occurs and that what it means to the individual.

Self-moving activities include movements of bodily organs, feelings, activities of needs, drives, wants, fear, hopes, thinking activities include all those functions that involve symbolic process of abstracting, conceptualising, speaking, writing, listening, asking questions, decision making, strategy formulation, etc. The electrochemical activities refer to bodily movements which begin with operation of DNA and RNA in the genes and includes neuronal activity. All these activities are interrelated and mutually dependent. Thus Self must be viewed as a unit which acts and reacts as a whole.

The environment as indicated in the model suggests that Self always moves in the context of environment. At times environment is close to the Self and limits the range of possible behavior, at other times it stretches for and does not exert great influence on the Self. The environment influences the Self and vice-versa.

The 'context environment' has four different dimensions which are basic and important: the physical dimension refers to the place we are, the social dimension to the type of functions we are attending — whether we are in a party, professional meeting, wedding, etc. The social dimension shows whether the environment is friendly, hostile, indifferent, etc. The cultural dimension suggests the prevailing value systems, the unwritten codes of acceptable or unacceptable behavior.

The Self functions in relation to 'time'. The Self operates in the present but with some reference to past experience and future envisions.

Thus Bois Model defines a human being as a thinking, feeling, self moving electrochemical organism in continuous interaction with a space-time environment.

Constraints of the Model: The model talks about only reacting to the environment but we react as well as act. Moreover Self and environment are not in clear cut contrast but they are in fluid interaction. The model is static whereas Self is constantly moving, changing and reorganising.

Thus we look at communication as exchange of semantic reactions.

There should be tacit recognition that both the parties are valuable and worthwhile to each other and have something important to contribute. Both parties should be allowed to convey and listen to messages and thus given opportunity to interact.

Homophily and hetrophily are significant for effective interpersonal communication. Homophily refers to degree of similarity between the parties engaged in interpersonal communication. Hetrophily refers to differences between the parties. Research evidence is that interpersonal communication is more effective when the parties are similar in age, gender, religion, socio-eco status, educational level and even professional and political leanings. But in certain communication situations, heterogeneity of the other parties becomes a necessary condition. Consider these two instances: when experts impart training, and diffusion process of innovations. In these two instances, change is often brought when the parties involved are 'optimally hetrophilious'.

Source credibility is important point for effective communication both for interpersonal and mass media. Source is seen as possessing or lacking credibility for its messages and interactions.

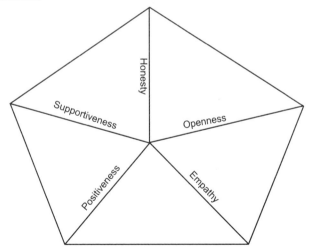

Fig. 1.28. Effective Interpersonal Communication Model

Society, Media and Audience Reciprocal Relationships

Mass media addresses the audience dependency on media

information that is ubiquitous condition in modern society. It is a key variable in understanding why and when media messages will alter beliefs, attitude and behavior and help maintain a sense of connectivity with social reality. Media operates in 'contextual environment', which varies in different societies.

The effectiveness of the communication through media channels depends on the reciprocal relationships between media, society and audience. The socio-economic, political, cultural and technological environments affect the media systems. The mass mediated messages aims at and creates awareness, knowledge and change in attitudes and behavior among the audience.

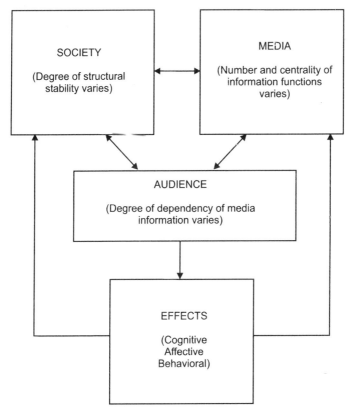

Fig. 1.29. Society, Media and Audience Reciprocal Relationships

DeFleur and Rokeach (1982) discuss the dependency theory of media effects. The proposition is that the potential for mass media messages to achieve a broad range of cognitive, affective, and behavioral effects will increase when media systems provide many unique and central information delivery services. The potential will further increase when there is structural instability due to conflict and change in society. The audience's changing cognitive, affective and behavioral conditions can give feedback to alter both society and media. Thus there is tripartite relationship between media, audience and society.

Figure 1.30 allows for a continuous process of interaction among society, media system and media audience. It is also a feedback model of effects of media messages on the audience in the sense that effects of ongoing events may set into motion another set of events. Most important is that this model avoids the position that media has no significant effect on audience and society or that media has unbounded capacity to manipulate people and society. Rather it allows us to specify in a limited way to say when and why media messages will or will not have significant effects on how audience thinks, feel and behave.

Media Effects. The characteristics of the media such as its goals, structure, organization, functions and operating policies affect the messages. Messages delivered in this particular framework can have desired or counter-desired effects depending on the characteristics of the audience.

For instance, TV in India is partially owned but wholly controlled by government. A few Indian private owned TV channels are allowed to operate but within the program content and other guidelines and control of Indian government. Government has the objective of being pro-social and its major function is to create information, knowledge, attitude and behavior changes for some of its major development programs; and to project its political and economic policies. Though in recent years to woo more audience and be in competition with private owned channels, it has changed its policies to deliver healthy entertainment programs also.

The media messages thus delivered by government or non-government channels construct the social realities of its people and people manage their social realities accordingly in a social set up where culture and society are not open. But in this age of globalization when people and particularly younger generation is exposed to global cultures and ways of life through TV messages and visuals there is conflict among people. They try to change or adopt to newer ways. The government is more concerned about foreign influence on the people's cultural ways and values and it takes action to control or censor.

Cognitive media effects occurs in three ways. First it is in terms of change in belief systems and attitudes and values. Second is media role in agenda setting. Agenda setting is an interactional process. The topics are selected by the media and presented to the public. Information about such topics is selectively assembled and selectively disseminated. The public sorts out the issues and information selectively. The list of issues that emerge is the agenda of media audience. Third is the expansion of people's system of beliefs. People's knowledge and belief system expands since they learn about other people, places and things from mass media.

Media has impact on values. Media information may not change the basic values but they play significant role in creating conditions for 'clarifying the values'. One way of clarifying such values is presenting information that precipitate value conflict within the audience. Once the mass mediated messages identify and clarify the value conflicts, the audience articulate their own value positions. In this process genuine values get clarified.

The affective effect of media messages is on audience feelings and emotions. For example, prolonged exposure to violence on media desensitizes people or creates fear and anxiety.

Forms of Communication

Interpersonal and Media are two basic forms of mass communication. There are different interpersonal and media

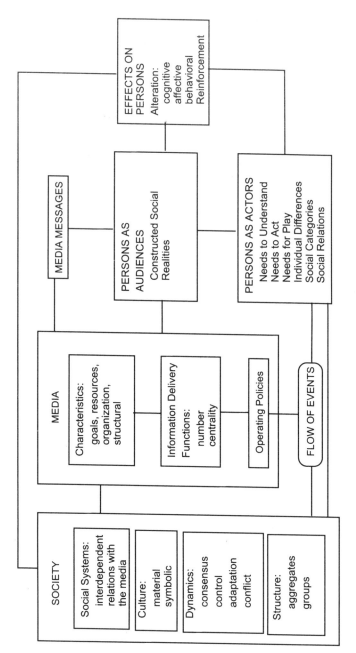

Fig. 1.30. Integrated Model of Media Effects

channels through which people communicate. There are four forms of interpersonal communication: intrapersonal, dyadic communication, small group communication and public speaking. The conventional mass communication channels are

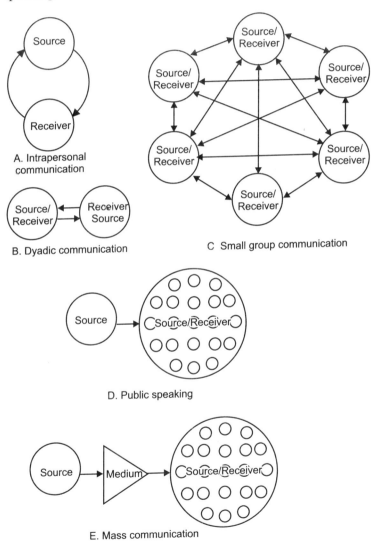

A. Intrapersonal communication

B. Dyadic communication

C Small group communication

D. Public speaking

E. Mass communication

Fig. 1.31. Forms of Communication

print, radio, TV, film, photography and exhibitions etc. With the advent of modern information communication technologies, other ethnotronic communication devices of video player and camcoder (video camera), audio players, audio and videocassettes and CDs have become ubiquitous and play supportive role for the conventional media channels. Telecommunication, Internet through world wide web and channelled through computer has become an important and significant channel of communication.

The basic models of communication evolved since 40s to 70s. These four decades of model development were crucial to the development of communication discipline. Research influenced the development of these models from a bullet theory premise to interactions, comprehensions and feedback loops in the models. It would be more appropriate to label them as foundation models in Communications discipline.

2

Development Communication (DEVCOM) Models

The dynamics and dysfunction of development have impeded or facilitated the devcom models operating in a particular society at a particular point of time. When the dynamics of development change, the devcom models undergo changes to fit the social, economic and political realities of the society and the global contexts in which they operate.

The various models given in this chapter are associated with Development Communication Perspective.

The focus of development has always been growth. In 50s and 60s, it was envisaged that economic growth could be through industrialization and modernization. Modernization presented the problems of social structural constraints. Lerner (1958) was the exemplar of modernization model. He pointed that urbanization, literacy and exposure to mass media are the indices of modernization.

Urbanization → Literacy → Economic and Political Participation

Mass Media Exposure

Fig. 2.1. Lerner Model of Development

The trickle down theory assumed that the benefits of industrialization and modernization would trickle down from rich to poor and from developed countries to developing countries.

Capital gain, and gain in awareness and knowledge would trickle down to poor from rich, and from developed countries to developing countries. But the theory did not work as assumed and rather created gap. The emphasis on mass media exposure created communication gap between the have and havenots because of limitations of media opportunities and media access. Urbanization created peripheral slum areas around urban metros and towns as rural population migrated to urban areas in search of employment opportunities and better quality of life. The efforts towards literacy were a slow process.

The dynamics of development are the patterns of interaction and social realities of various agents of development. Political leadership, development administration, rural and urban masses are the agents of development. The major dynamic factor for development is 'development efforts' by all the agents. Development efforts comprise of development awareness, motivation for development and participation in development.

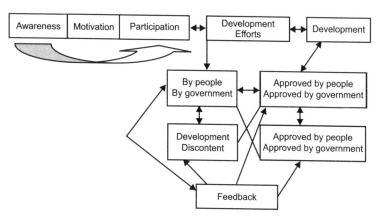

Fig. 2.2. Dynamics of Development Communication

There is relationship between development awareness, discontent, motivation and feedback linkages with participation, approval and adoption of development projects.

The analysis of six development decades suggests that development discontents in the developing countries were created by the interaction patterns of the development agents.

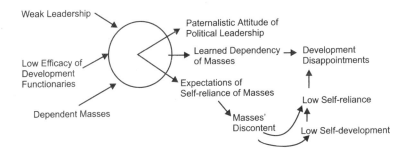

Fig. 2.3. Dysfunctional Factors in Development

The above figure shows that coordination was not achieved among people's participation, local leadership and effective development administration. The 'affordances' of the social system resulted in weak local leadership, ineffective functionaries in the development bureaucracy and masses that remained dependent. Though they shifted their dependence from the local community to the central government. The government's goal to improve the material wellbeing of the masses within a context of democratic socialism is difficult and contains some unresolved contradictory tensions.

Discontent and personal inefficacy are serious concerns for development because they make all the participants in development describe themselves as helpless in achieving the development objective, make people blame each other and withdraw from commitment to democratic participation in development.

Pervasive discontent with development program is a problem if it leads to withdrawal from participation but otherwise discontent *per se* need not be a problem. It would rather motivate to achieve the development objectives.

The assumption is that future development programs are built as a result of interactions between people and social-economic-technological opportunities. Once we gain a deeper understanding of the directions of change, we may define with greater measure of confidence our region of feasible action as shown in Fig. 2.4.

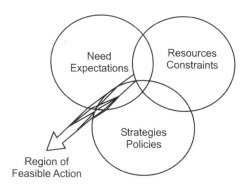

Fig. 2.4. Region of Feasible Action

Development communication needs and expectations are subjective categories. There are three sets of problems related to it: (i) there are behavior orientations related to all media, (ii) affective orientation with regard to major national development communication expectations, needs and constraints of resources, (iii) cognitive orientations with respect to major national development communication strategies and policies.

Development threshold concept suggests being receptive to development to a certain point. For example, there is a marked difference between the development threshold of rural and urban society, between elite and masses, and even men and women within rural and urban society. These differences in threshold are termed as 'development gap'. The development gap hypothesis is that patterns of communication may lead the have-nots away from the mainstream of development and thus create development gap.

This also suggests that people at different development thresholds need different communication strategies for effective development. Human and localized approach suggests communication efforts tailored to the needs and psychological dispositions of people.

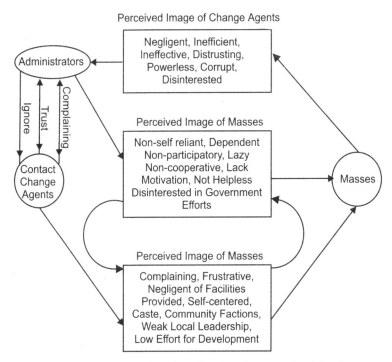

Fig. 2.5. Communication Gap for Development Participation

Development Effort is identified with what activates people to participate in development. The development effort is further defined as development awareness, development discontent, and motivation for participation in development programs.

Fig. 2.6. Development Efforts
Source: Narula: Dynamics of Development

The development awareness addresses the question of people's awareness of development programs in general and specific activities going on in the local areas or likely to be taken in future. The general awareness is identified with interest and arousal stage, whereas specific awareness is identified with participation and adoption stage. The extent of awareness as high and low depends on source, content and credibility of communication links.

Development discontent is multidimensional. The discontent could occur with the existing development and communication strategies. People get discontented when people's development demands are not met. The assumption is that development discontent activates people to participate aggressively in development.

Development motivation for participation is identified with the demands of the people made on the government or other agencies for satisfying development needs. Such motivation also stimulate people to take self or community initiative to do development. The motivational force for development may be the psychological arousal of people. Awareness, knowledge of the issues and reasons and patterns of discontentment are necessary and sufficient for motivation.

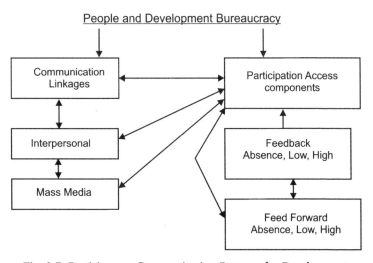

Fig. 2.7. Participatory Communication Patterns for Development

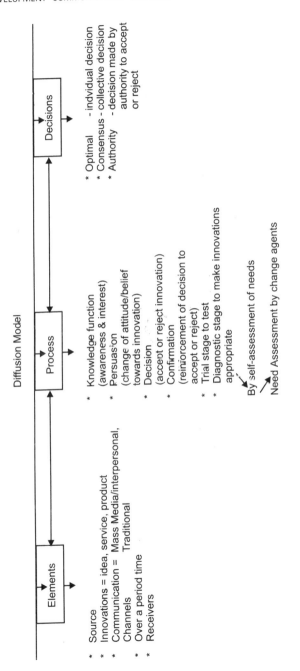

Diffusion Model

Elements

* Source
* Innovations = idea, service, product
* Communication = Mass Media/interpersonal,
  Channels   Traditional
* Over a period time
* Receivers

Process

* Knowledge function
  (awareness & interest)
* Persuasion
  (change of attitude/belief
  towards innovation)
* Decision
  (accept or reject innovation)
* Confirmation
  (reinforcement of decision to
  accept or reject)
* Trial stage to test
* Diagnostic stage to make innovations
  appropriate

By self-assessment of needs

Need Assessment by change agents

Decisions

* Optimal   - individual decision
* Consensus - collective decision
* Authority - decision made by
               authority to accept
               or reject

Fig. 2.8. Roger's Basic Diffusion Model

Development participation happens with the individual and community initiated participation in local development activities in the past, present and to do so in the future. The degree of involvement is identified with the frequency with which people discuss development. The forms and the modes of participation differ considerably in different societies reflecting local, economic, political and social variables.

What, who and how of participation is augmented by consideration of how the context of participation may affect its extent and substance. Analysis of the development task and the salient features of development environment may make the context explicit.

Diffusion of Innovations is the adoption of technological and social innovations through diffusion of new ideas, services and products. Diffusion of both material and social innovations is necessary for development. The individual and community decisions for acceptance and rejection of innovations depend primarily on the needs of the adopters, what is communicated about innovation, and how it is communicated.

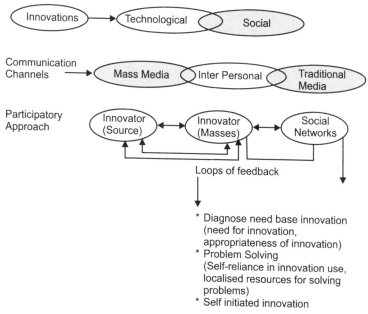

Fig. 2.9. Diffusion — A Communication Strategy for Development

The three important stages in such communication are: create awareness by *reorienting* the products, services by introducing the changed innovative elements. Creating knowledge and interest by *refocusing* the attention on the innovations. Further, innovative ideas have to be *reinforced* by both intensive and extensive media and interpersonal campaigns. The reinforcement helps in making decisions and adoptions.

The notion of how development works in developing countries. The development planners have a definite notion of how the various groups should interact to bring about development. They envision all agents as actively participating in a fully circular process. In this process, their own role is that of providing expertise that guides the action of others.

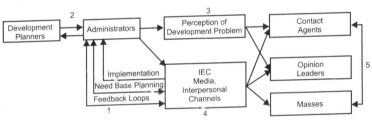

Fig. 2.10. Planners' Concept of How Development Works

The administrative change agents blame the masses for the failure of development projects, citing their passive participation. The pattern of actions and attributions made by the administrative change agents is shown in Fig. 2.10.

There is a complex and now familiar pattern of interaction between the administrators and the masses. The administrators are frustrated because they do not have adequate resources to provide all the services the masses need. The combination of assumed responsibility, inadequate provision of services and expressed frustration elicits a complex response by the masses, including a high degree of development awareness, discontent and dependency. There is rapid, reiterated cycle of exchanges in which each blames the other.

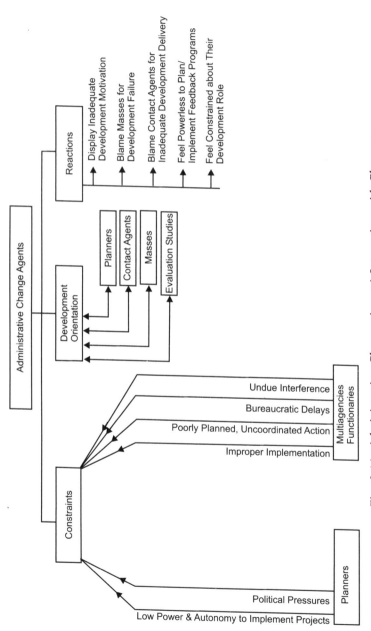

Fig. 2.11. Administrative Change Agents' Interaction with Planners

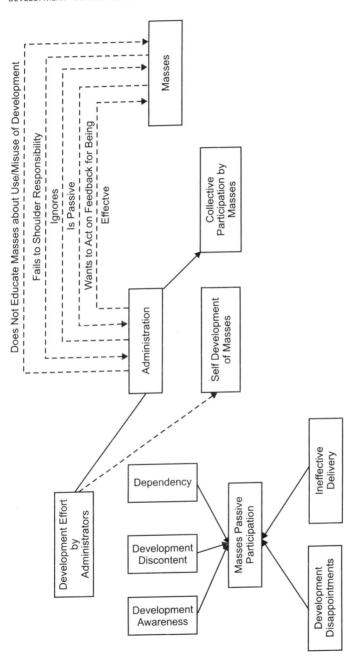

Fig. 2.12. Administrative Change Agents' Interaction with Masses

Fatalism	Characteristics Perceived as Problems	Government Intentions	Development Efforts	Actual Effects
Contentment	Yes	Improved quality	Motivate (e.g., create discontentment with things as they are)	Discontentment
Dependency	No	—	—	Dependency (on the government rather than on fate, landlords or social hierarchy)
Unaware of innovations	Yes	Inform	Educate	Aware of innovations
Exploited	Yes	Emancipate	Legislate protective policies: inform people of rights	Well informed of personal rights; an attitude of having been victimized and now entitled to unearned benefits. The government offered itself as paternalistic; to the extent that development communication is successful, people take the role of clients.
Participation limited to the local social hierarchy	Yes	Develop the individual or prossessing identity and rights	Intrude into existing hierarchies with radio, TV and personnel linking individuals to the government	Learned dependency; participation consists of accepting things offered as owed, and of "complaining" (that is, "informing the government that it its not doing its job.")

Table 2.13. Effects of Development Communication Programs

Development dialogue focuses on application of policy skills, development of administrative infrastructure, communication infrastructure and dialogue strategies. Participatory development and good governance are necessary conditions for dialogue for development. The emphasis is on micro level action contexts, local resistance to change, community participation, and empowerment of people through participation. Simple, moral, accountable, responsible and transparent (SMART) government is advocated for development. With the two components of participation and good governance; strategies can be built around the development issues to reach a consensus to do development. In this context, the government knows people's needs and the people know limitations of the government; and they agree to do development within this framework of partnership.

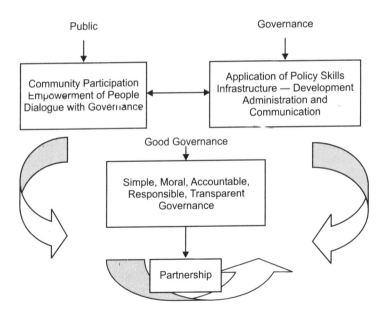

Fig. 2.14. Development Dialogue Strategies

The basic model of development suggests the various components of development and its dynamics that are discussed above in specific contexts.

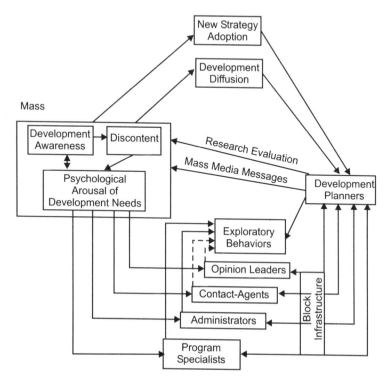

Fig. 2.15. Development: Basic Model

3

International Communication and Globalization Models

International Communication is sending messages to international community. It may cross the physical boundaries of countries or without that. People are talking to other people in different countries on phones, on Internet and through video-conferences etc. without leaving their homes or work places. They communicate about themselves through content messages on TV, radio, or cinema. People communicate face-to-face with the people when they visit those countries and places. Letters, books, newspapers from one country may cross over to other countries and they communicate about people's concerns, their cultures and life styles.

Messages could be oral, written, visual or action. One or many may receive the message through one or multi-channels. The form may be products, services, infrastructures and ideas. Senders could be individuals (one on one), group organizations, governments, and international organizations from different countries. Channels could be multimedia and interpersonal. Message may be issue-specific or interest evoking issues.

The important components of the model are: interaction with different countries and nations. It is important that the messages are of interest to both senders and receivers. Both media technologies and interpersonal channels are used to facilitate communication. Noise element is incomprehension of what sender wants to convey till it is brought to the level where receiver is able to comprehend for further feedback and action. Circular communication is essential since main objective in many instances is to reach mutual understanding. Therefore, feedback, reaction is sought on the messages conveyed which could be both positive and negative depending on the circumstances. In the model given below the first and the fourth components i.e. interaction and comprehension of the message are the most important.

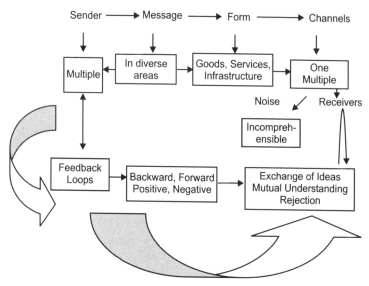

Fig. 3.1. Nature of International Communication

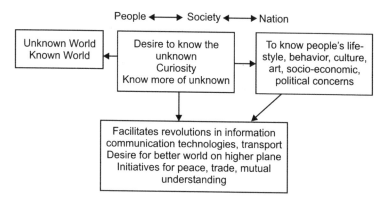

Fig. 3.2. Key Factors in International Communication

Television shows us life styles of people from different lands, their varied socio-cultural, political concerns. There is instant feeling that their behavior, values are totally different or somewhat different. The print media also reflect these dimensions. The curiosity to know these dimensions better and to integrate those cultural practices stimulate us to communicate and interact with people in other countries through personal or impersonal, interpersonal and media channels.

The deliberations of 'Right to information' debates of 70s-80s of MaCBride commission led to the 'New World Information and Communication Order' (NWICO). Where it was advocated that developing countries should have the right to present information about their countries in the global context. They should have control over their communication channels. The international flow of information would be restructured to allow a balance of communication power between western countries and developing nations.

Absence of a consensus on the shape of a 'New world information and communication order' demonstrates that we are in an age of paradigm shifts. Our political and economic institutions are clearly lagging behind the accelerating pace of scientific, technological and cultural change. For international relations, the significant change is through expansion of global communication.

NWICO can be best constructed by developing communication competence for the voiceless. Pluralism in voices however requires pluralism in structures of media access. No single system of media control (governmental, commercial, public, or community) can alone guarantee the plurality of voices. A balance among them might use the expanding channels of communication for an expanding plurality of voices more reflective of the international community.

It calls for free and balanced flow of information among the billions inhabitants of this world, who are caught up between the imperatives of pre-modern, modern, and postmodern worlds to which they belong. NWICO may be conceived of as a network of networks of NGOs, to mobilize the global civil society, to empower the urban and the rural communities, to enhance their communication competence and media capabilities, to negotiate with the State and Non-State actors to redress their conditions.

Global Communication is imperative these days to connect to people globally not only on just one on one basis but across many countries because of growing needs and demands on many fronts viz. political, economic, socio-cultural, technology etc. A network of communication across countries, inter-country and cross-country leads to globalization. Several countries communicate at bilateral or multilateral levels on specific issues.

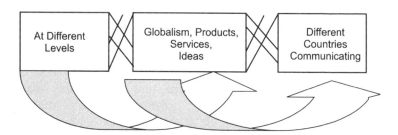

Fig. 3.3. Global Communication Model

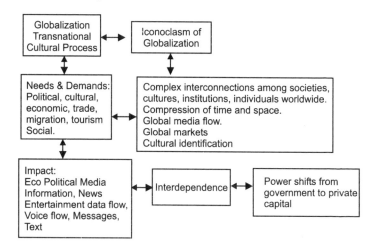

Fig. 3.4. Globalization Contexts

Globalization Contexts. The frequent inter-country and cross-country interactions depend on their (each country's) needs and demand to interact. These could be economic including trade, political, technology, cultural, migration, social and tourism. The forces of interdependence of nations do create a close knit global economy and other systems. The force of globalization shifts power away from governments to private capital. ICTs have been the main driving force and facilitator in all these contexts.

Interdependency Model addresses the issue of international interdependency for international development and resolving crucial issues of political conflicts and war. Communication is an important component.

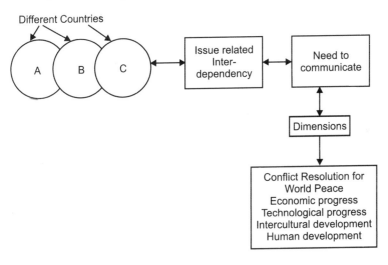

Fig. 3.5. **Global Interdependency Model**

Technological breakthroughs, innovations, re-inventions are researched and developed by many countries' scientists and technologists. Ultimately the end product may be achieved and patented by one country but the ultimate objective is to let all benefit by it whether it is telephone, electricity, television, radio, computer etc. The ICTs of present decade suggest global networking. Whether it is e-mail through computer, varied uses of telecommunications or broadcasting, and use of satellites. These ICTs work when there are global interconnected efforts for both hardware and software. These do not exist or survive by the efforts of a single country.

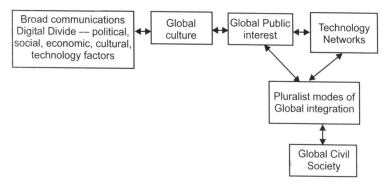

Fig. 3.6. Global Technology Networking Communication Model-1

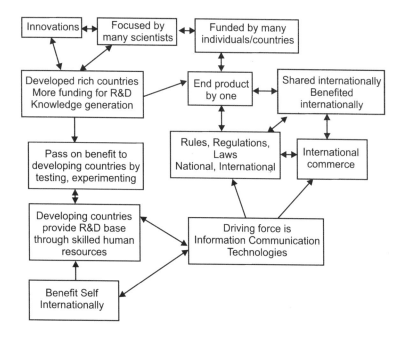

Fig. 3.7. Global Technology Networking Communication Model-2

4

Information Communication Technology (ICT) Models

Information resources, national policies, needs and demands for information technology interact to create specific information environment, culture and models. These are universal concerns for ICTs. But there are models within the framework of these universal concerns, which are very specific to each country when applied. This is evidenced by case study research.

In the last six decades the communication revolutions in ICTs have impacted the social and working lives of people around the world.

Every change in ICTs throughout human history has produced anxious voices. There have been dilemmas of innovations.

Social technologies are imperative for the diffusion of communication technologies. The concept of social technology is acceptance of a particular medium as well as the message meaning relayed through the individual and the social system. The performance demands of technology must fit into existing patterns of human interactions to be meaningful in the particular social system and must meet the standards of their social traditions that act as guideline for acceptance, rejection and censorship both by government and the people. The adoption of technology is a social decision so it has social implications.

The salient examples are computer and video technologies in India from 90s to date. In India, the adoption of computer was resisted in 90s. It had gone through the stages of anxiety, fear and apprehensions of losing jobs. In 2000 decades it is now well accepted and ubiquitous. In 90s the video was accepted as an inexpensive means of entertainment through video parlors. Indian government has to censor the video entertainment for its misuse.

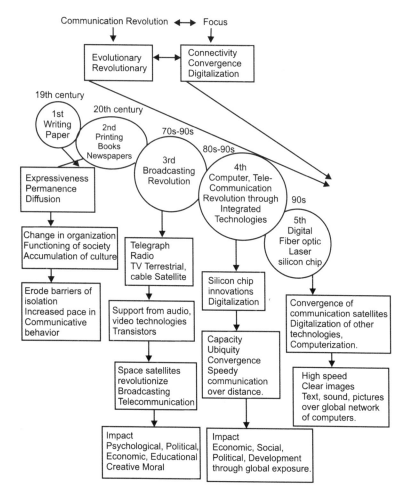

Fig. 4.1. Communication Technology Revolutions

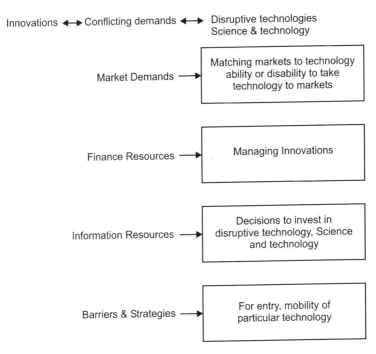

Fig. 4.2. Dilemmas of Innovations

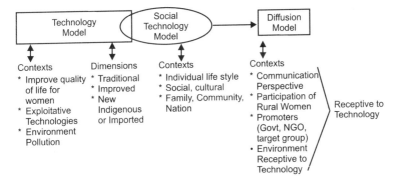

Fig. 4.3. Technology Promotion Model

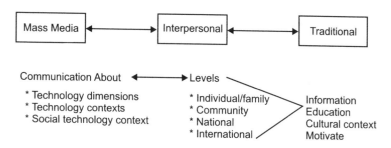

Fig. 4.4. Technology Perspective Model

In Fig. 4.5, change is positioned between traditional and other current factors that influence development. The change 'wheel' is not an even one; it changes shape according to the centrifugal and centripetal forces exerted by other dynamics as the wheel turns. At some time the wheel spins more rapidly than at other times. At times, more change is felt by some factors than others. One certainty is that all factors (traditional and current) will experience some aspect or effect of change.

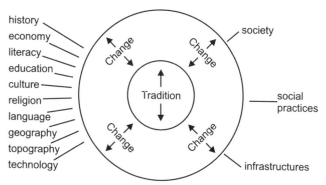

Fig. 4.5. Components of Change

The determinants for communication technology could be cultural determinants, value assumptions, cultural resources and acceptance of ICTs.

There are two important dimensions of technology diffusion. On one hand, there is interaction of scientific and technical factors; and on the other hand, there is interaction of economic, social, and political factors. The overall 'interaction points' of these two dimensions determine technological development, its applications, and communication.

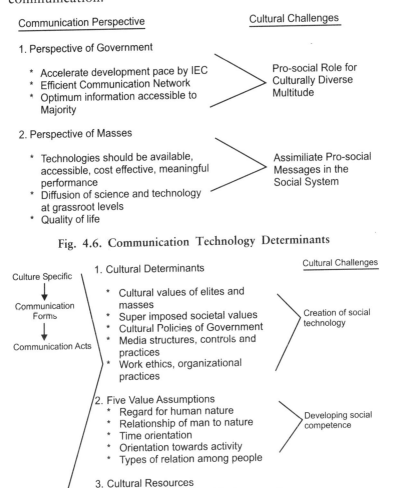

Communication Perspective   **Cultural Challenges**

1. Perspective of Government

    * Accelerate development pace by IEC
    * Efficient Communication Network
    * Optimum information accessible to Majority

Pro-social Role for Culturally Diverse Multitude

2. Perspective of Masses

    * Technologies should be available, accessible, cost effective, meaningful performance
    * Diffusion of science and technology at grassroot levels
    * Quality of life

Assimiliate Pro-social Messages in the Social System

Fig. 4.6. Communication Technology Determinants

Culture Specific
↓
Communication Forms
↓
Communication Acts

1. Cultural Determinants   Cultural Challenges

    * Cultural values of elites and masses
    * Super imposed societal values
    * Cultural Policies of Government
    * Media structures, controls and practices
    * Work ethics, organizational practices

Creation of social technology

2. Five Value Assumptions
    * Regard for human nature
    * Relationship of man to nature
    * Time orientation
    * Orientation towards activity
    * Types of relation among people

Developing social competence

3. Cultural Resources
    * Language, Religion, Ideology
    * Values, Ways of doing and Making things
    * Myths, Stories, Artifacts
    * Typifications, Interpretative procedures

Putting cultural resources at risk

4. Accept Technology - Challenges related to 1,2,3 are accepted

Cultural–LAG

Fig. 4.7. Communication Technology Determinants–Integrated

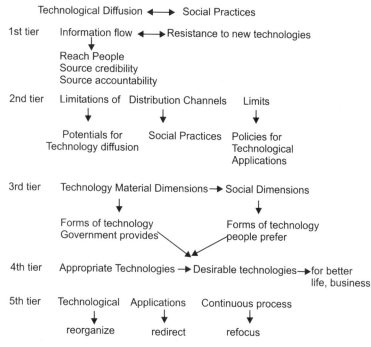

Fig. 4.8. Diffusion of Technology Tiers

When society is using Advance Information Technology in its varied applications; it focuses on varied dimensions to make information technology effective.

Rapid technological change, unpredictability of consumer demands, and diversity of innovative applications have created much uncertainty about the speed of development and diffusion; and economic, social, and cultural impact.

Social research can refine understanding of the complex roles that social, organizational and cultural processes play in the development of ICTs in various sectors of society. Yet the complexities and interdependencies of technological, organizational, and social change make prescriptions for policies and practice highly problematic and contingent on the special and historical context.

The social process of ICTs and its effect on the society

represents a new perspective on social and behavioral processes. They seek guidance through research to improve social interventions using technology in domains such as education, mental health, work productivity etc. Scientists and technologists highlight the human side of electronic communications and they think about the social processes and effects of ICTs designs, applications and policies.

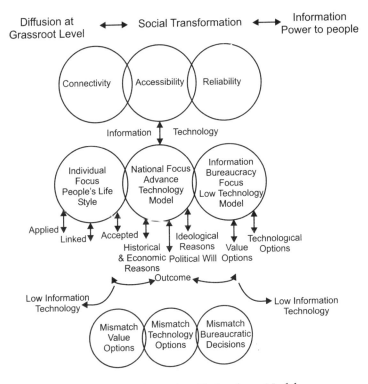

Fig. 4.9. Information Technology Model

Every society differs in the race for information technology and building of information society. The general model provides background to information technology efforts.

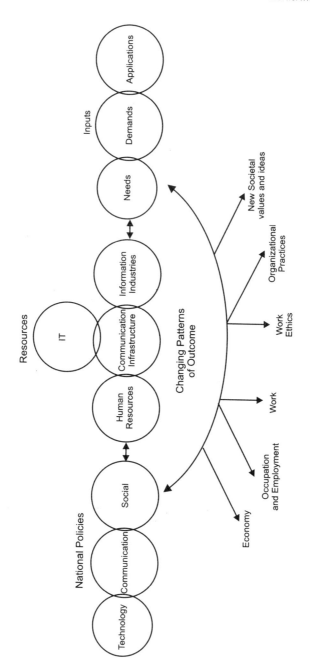

Fig. 4.10. Advance Information Technology Model

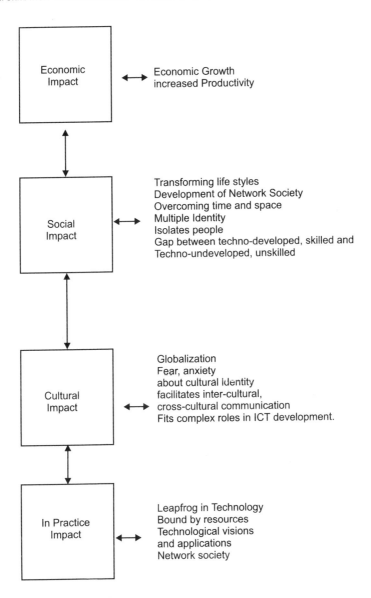

Fig. 4.11. Information Technology Impact

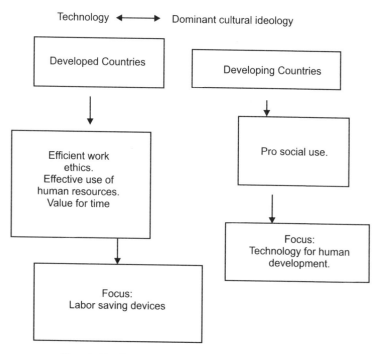

Fig. 4.12. **Communication Technology Contexts**

Fig 4.13 suggests that the development of information society depends on the interplay of resources, national policies and inputs. When these factors interact, the outcome is the changing patterns of economy, occupations and employment, work and work ethics, and organizational practices. The changing patterns result in new societal values and ideas.

The information society develops to the advance stage through development of information technology culture and its diffusion. This has impact on national and international levels and facilitates gaining power.

Management of information causes increasing problems for the organizations: (i) how to make a whole of the scattered information, (ii) how to screen out relevant information, (iii) how to extract from the information environment those messages likely to have significance for the organization. Two important communication skills are needed in this context: Knowledge Management and Impression Management.

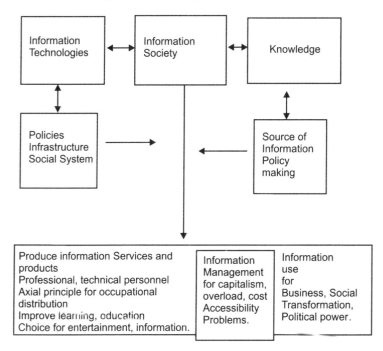

Fig. 4.13. Information Society: General Model

Knowledge management of scientific information helps in innovations. Management of other kinds of information helps in decision-making and leadership roles. Impression management is needed for visual professional competence. It is the direct visual impression that creates the illusion of credibility and not visual information itself. Advertising and marketing industries work hard to find more and more effective visual means of impression management.

Digitalization is another technological possibility that offers a universal system that is distributed through satellite or through fiber optics. Digitalization of information makes the same channel of communications more useful by doubling up on the amounts of information carried through conventional conduits.

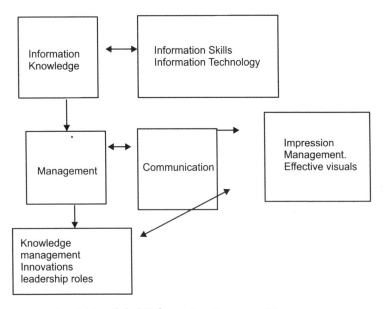

Fig. 4.14. Global Information Economy Management

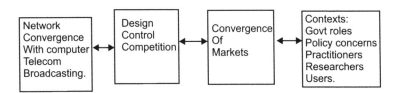

Fig. 4.15. Digital Convergence

The potential impact of digital convergence is on the pre-digital media system of print, film, radio, television, computer and telecommunications. Production technology has become more computer-based and is creating new media forms. Technological and economic drivers of such convergence will have social, cultural and economic impacts. The policy concern, players and stakes will be different in each context.

Internet is fast expanding and is ubiquitous in all walks of life. It is having tremendous impact on people's life and how the businesses are being conducted and has facilitated globalization. Information gathering, sharing is the major focus and much is achieved through it. Internet is a *New World* for social behavior.

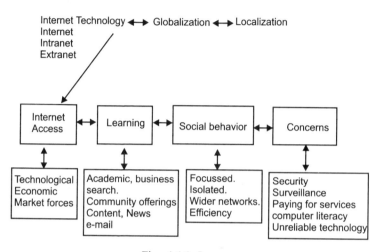

Fig. 4.16. Internet

Presently, there is multimedia approach to ICTs. The convergence of mainstream ICTs and supporting ICT, and an integrated approach to information technologies is having social, cultural and economic impact on the lifestyle and societies globally.

Information technology is important for globalization process. It has impact on globalization and vice versa. Importance of information and ICTs addresses three concerns: the liberalization of markets, encouragement of competition between different systems, and the globalization process in the context of third world.

The powerful flow of information, news, and various broadcasting programs not only saturate the world markets but are also having tremendous impact on people's life.

Complex process of global interconnectedness, time-space compression and action at distance re-envisaged the world. This creates iconoclasm of globalization. Transculturation, hybridization, and indigenization are important in understanding the cultural influences. These rethink of cultural

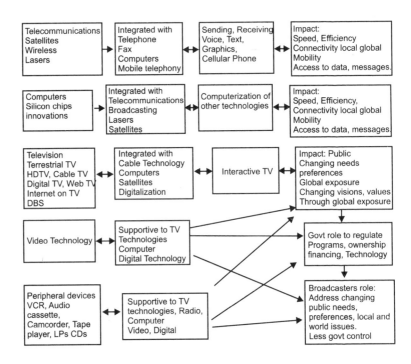

Fig. 4.17. Information Technologies: Integrated Approach

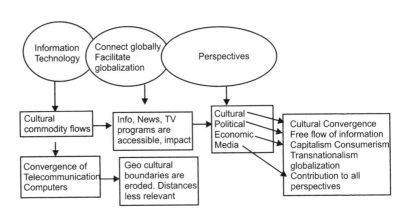

Fig. 4.18. Globalization of Technology

power not as cultural imperialism but as a process of cultural integration. The communication in global contexts presents cultural challenges.

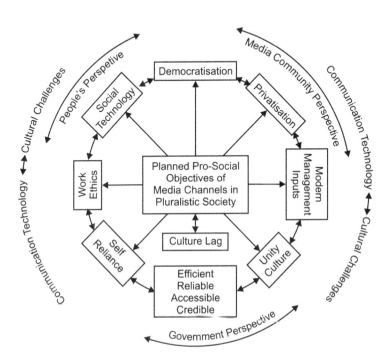

Fig. 4.19. Communication Technology and Cultural Challenges

Technology is a component of culture and is understood in its cultural context and the choice of technology is within this system. Communication technology presents cultural challenges. It poses cultural challenges for preserving or destroying the cultural identity and values of a particular society. It can pose challenges for cultural vitality, diversity and intercultural understanding. These challenges are also culture-specific.

5

Intercultural Communication Models

All cultural models suggest *Diversity* and *Unity*. There is unity in diversity. The cultural models are grouped in two classes: the models in immigrant societies that essentially comprise of heterogeneous cultures and the models operating in homogeneous societies.

Culture and communication has been defined in variety of ways both by culture academicians and practitioners. Both are basic and necessary components of intercultural communication. The cultural models in immigration societies such as Melting Pot model, Cross-cultural Images model, Multi-culture model, and Trans-culture model highlight the diversity, cultural influences, and contexts. These create intercultural tensions and multiculturalism.

Figure 1 'Communication Perspective' given in introduction chapter in context of cultural communication suggests that the particular forms of communication shape the social institutions and social traditions. People interpret their environments and experiences. People derive their power of communication from their resources of cultural habits and practices. They reconstitute and reinterpret them when faced with alien culture and interact with coordination and coherence.

The contact situation is viewed in terms of ecological contexts and the demographic characteristics of people. The patterns of conjunctive relations are envisaged in terms of intercultural role networks. The cultural (acculturation) process includes several sub-processes such as intercultural transmission (diffusion), cultural creativity, cultural disintegration, and reactive adaptations. Cultural fusion, assimilation, and a stabilizing pluralism are the lasting outcome of acculturation.

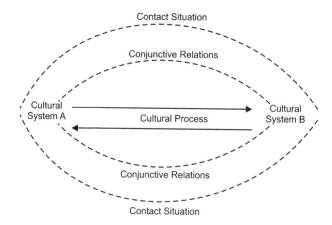

Fig. 5.1. Approach to Cultural Communication

The model subsumes the effects of pre-migration factors, and situational determinants in the receiving society. These are concerned with socio-psychological aspects. Length of residence in the receiving society is taken as an independent variable that interacts with both pre-migration and situational determinants to modify the objectives and subjective modes of adaptation.

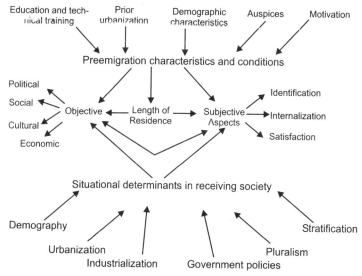

Fig. 5.2. Multivariate Model for Immigration Adaptation Process

The model given below reflects how socio-demographic characteristics and various communication variables involved in the process of acculturation of ethnic groups function and interact with one another to facilitate or impede acculturation.

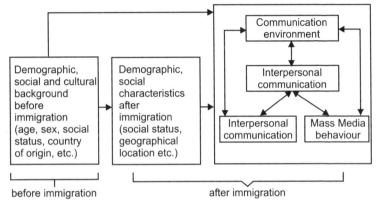

Fig. 5.3. Communication Model for Acculturation

Technology and media connectivity not only exposes people to cultural ways and cultural diversity but it also diffuses the same to a global audience and shape unique cultural ways. The interaction of culture specific images of self and others, stereotypes, prejudices, multicultural settings and media exposure create Intercultural Images which are further facilitated by social communication networks, and intercultural communication competence for wider political, social, economic, business, and technological ramifications.

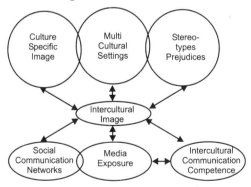

Fig. 5.4. Cultural Diffusion: Intercultural Image

Communication technologies are apparatuses through which cultural invasion and cultural domination may take place. This may in turn create cultural dilemmas, crisis of cultural identities, and related tensions. The dynamics are how the cultural diversity is managed.

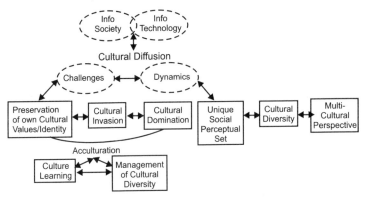

Fig. 5.5. Cultural Diffusion: Challenges and Dynamics

This figure below presents a holistic viewpoint of cultural diffusion from the point of various milieu and communication variables.

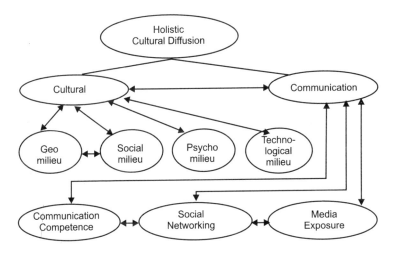

Fig. 5.6. Cultural Diffusion: Integrated Perspective

The major prospect of cultural diffusion is in its being the agent of intercultural change, intercultural understanding and political peace. Intercultural change depends on human communication environments, intercultural contexts, technologies and the immigration policies. The right type of information, knowledge about various cultures can create intercultural understanding and in turn political peace. Political and economic demands and expectations created by intercultural contexts create constraints for cultural diffusion.

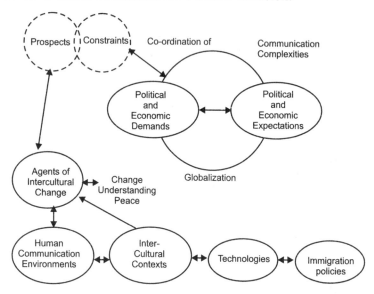

Fig. 5.7. Cultural Diffusion: Prospects and Constraints

Take the instance of the phenomenon of globalization as an effort for women development at various levels and through various focuses. This has implications for global visibility, transparency and development strategies for women. The participation of individual countries in international conferences and agreements means that nations expose themselves for comparisons with other nations. Transparency at the international levels suggests that abuses at the national level are more visible and more embarrassing to the governments. That many governments over the world appear to be willing to commit to women's rights and gender equality.

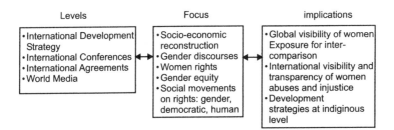

Fig. 5.8. International Strategies for Women Development

We observe that every culture-society differs in the race for information technology and building of information society. Beside technology, the cultural resources and practices play significant role in these efforts. We do face the communication challenges in cultural contexts. A cultural perspective in globalization addresses how cultural diffusion can facilitate globalization. Conflicts are generated through complexities in cultures.

6

Communication Management Models

Communication is an important component in every human activity. It is effective when it is managed well. Therefore it is important how communication is managed in various streams for effective delivery of ideas, products, and services. The

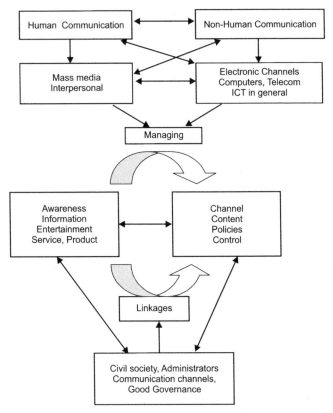

Fig. 6.1. Communication Management Competence

management could be of both human and non-human (computer, telecommunication etc) communications. In fact, management of knowledge is the significant component in communication management.

Management approach calls for holistic approach to communication in any particular area, be it business, entertainment, information technology or development. The necessary conditions for such a holistic approach are IECM strategies, linkages between civil society, administrators and communication channels, and good governance. Management competency is important.

Business Communication Models

The focus of business communication is on diverse dimensions of businesses. The various Business Communication Models take four approaches. First is general approach to business communications. Second is special approach that handles business communications from various perspectives in specific aspects of different business sectors. Some of these may include negotiations in business dealings, management of products and services, product-cycle, advertisement and public relations, globalization, information technology, training (including intercultural training) etc. and overall effective communications.

The third approach focuses on communications for human relations in businesses. These include employee relation management (ERM), customer relation management (CRM), product relation management (PRM) etc. Fourth approach focuses on business and economic intelligence and analysis, economics of business communications.

Business intelligence and its social components, changing dimensions and areas of businesses, and the new and wider applications of ICTs create a specific business culture for a particular business. Communications through conventional and new media technologies, and interpersonal channels play significant role in managing these three business communication components. Internet and various modes of mobile communications have facilitated global business and globalization in business. Through newer technologies of Internet we are stepping into e-commerce.

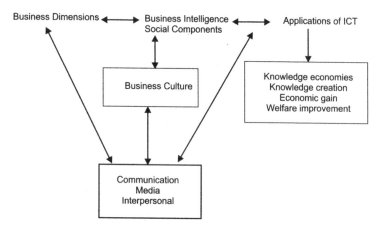

Fig. 6.2. Business Communication Management

Managing knowledge economy for economic gain through business and economic growth culminating in improvement of welfare is important. It is the efficient use of knowledge in this context.

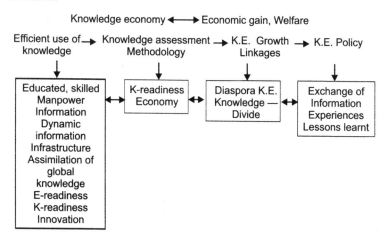

Fig. 6.3. Managing Knowledge Economies

Knowledge as an important component of communications that needs management for its effective use in varied sectors of activity. This model addresses the issues of knowledge management competencies and dynamics, various components, applications, techniques, and its impact on number of variables.

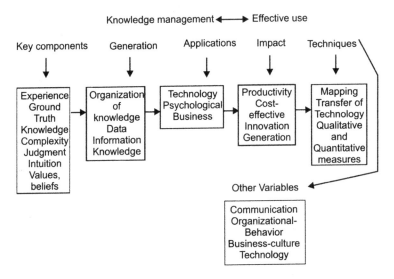

Fig. 6.4. Knowledge Management Model

Conflict Management Models

The figures given below deal with conflict process, variables of conflict, and the conflict resolution efforts through conflict management. Efforts of various stakeholders manage conflicting information to achieve balance and justice.

Fig. 6.5. Conflict Management Model

Conflict is a process and it erupts when there is a saturation point pertaining to certain variables. The two models given below map the variables in conflict when there is disturbed peace crisis. Peace dimensions design helps in conflict resolution.

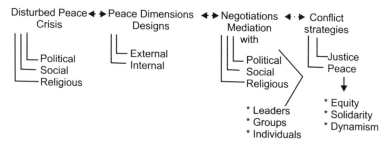

Fig. 6.6. Conflict Process Model

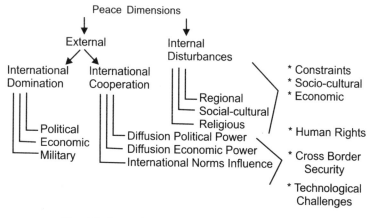

Fig. 6.7. Peace Dimensions for Conflict Resolution

The national and international conflicts are triggered by many variables. National conflicts can culminate in international conflicts. Therefore, the preliminary steps taken by stakeholders is to resolve national conflicts both for the sake of national-conflicts *per se* and for international conflicts.

The triggering of conflicts with its issues and consequences, its escalation and de-escalation is modelled. Further, when the social conflicts are protracted, certain dynamics are significant.

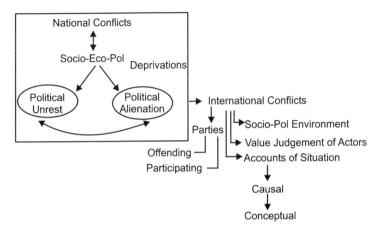

Fig. 6.8. Conflict Variables Model

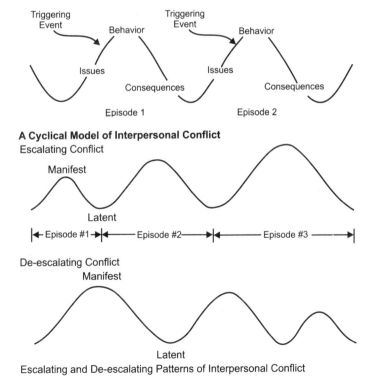

Fig. 6.9. Diagnostic Model of Interpersonal Conflict

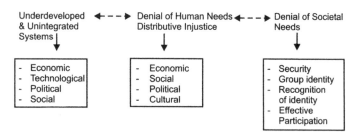

Fig. 6.10. Dynamics of Protracted Social Conflicts

Third party intervention and communication can help
resolve the conflicts. The four components — aggression,
conflict, negotiations, order and peaceful change manipulate
the parties for conflict resolution.

Understanding conflict dynamics helps in conflict
management. The conflict dynamics are issues, triggering events,
resolution initiatives and consequences.

Purposes of Conflict Dialogue		
Elements of Conflict Cycle or Episode	Diagnostic Objectives	Action Objectives
1. Issues in conflict	Differentiate basic from symptomatic issues and resolvable from unresolvable issues	Resolve by compromise or integration of substantive differences and working through of emotional differences
2. Events or conditions that trigger manifest conflict	Identify barriers to conflict or conflict management behaviours and events that precipitate such behaviour	Control by avoiding triggering new episode unless constructive purpose will be served
3. Manifest tactics or resolution initiatives	Understand how characteristic conflict behaviours can generate additional issues	Control by limiting destructive tactics, encouraging constructive initiatives
4. Consequences, including feelings produced by conflict	Understand the feelings generated by conflict episodes how they are coped with, and therefore whether they are fueling the next episode	Control by assisting principals to cope better with feelings and other consequences of conflict

Table 6.11. Conflict Dynamics and Conflict Management

Figure given below presents an integrated model to manage conflicts. Conflict resolution requires integrated efforts of parties in conflict focusing on flexibility of attitudes, dialogue among the parties, negotiations and action taken accordingly. Even for negotiated actions it is necessary to make integrated efforts by both the parties.

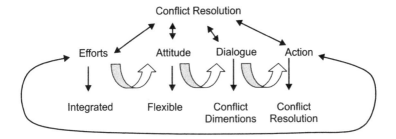

Fig. 6.12. Conflict Resolution Integrated Model

7

Business Communication Practices Models

There are community initiatives that use the Internet and other digital communication networks and people networks to access markets, skills and opportunities to derive real economic benefits. Business communication framework focuses on perspectives, types of communication, contexts and patterns. It defines the scope, concepts and essential components of business communications and its tools. It presents the salient models of Business Communications.

Communication in any business operates from three perspectives: One, customer-supply chain relationships including both external and internal links; two, employee-management relationship including internal links only and customer-consumer-product relationships.

The dynamics of business communications are customer-supplier relationships in the context of product, services and people. Communications occurs in different forms in these relationships. It may be a set of data, information or knowledge about product, services and about people. These may be conveyed through technology, media, and oral interpersonal or through written word. The employee-management relationship is in the context of performance, productivity and human relations. These may be assessed and conveyed through technology, media, and oral interpersonal or through written word. But in addition, the human relations approach of developing reciprocal good attitude and behavior to create good and healthy work environments and professional development is important to assess and boost the performance and productivity in any business organization.

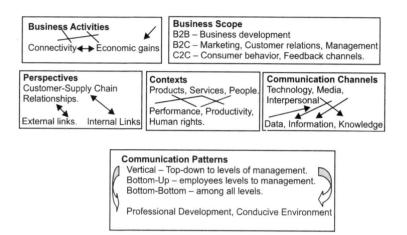

Fig. 7.1. Business Communication Framework

Business Communication Models

We may understand the business concepts well but in practice it is important to manage the business reality well. Communication strategies are one of the components to manage business reality. The focus of business communication is on diverse dimensions of businesses. The various Business Communication Models take seven approaches. First is general approach to business communications. Second is special approach that handles business communications from various perspectives in specific aspects of different business sectors. Some of these may include negotiations in business dealings, marketing and management of products and services, product-cycle, advertisement and public relations, globalization and information technology. Third approach is communications for employee–management relationships in the context of development of business and professional development of people. It may be achieved through dialogue strategies among all levels in the organization, through training, coaching, mentoring and candid and frequent appraisals.

The fourth approach focuses on communications for human relations in businesses. These include employee relation management (ERM), customer relation management (CRM), product relation management (PRM) and resource management. Fifth approach focuses on business and economic intelligence and analysis, and economics of business communications. Sixth approach is the segmented market focus on the poor and those having low level purchasing capability. This presents co-creation Business Model. This is the recent new business model. So far the marketers have ignored this segment though in many developing countries, this segment comprises almost 70% of the market. Seventh approach is the business communication to rural markets. This segment also forms almost 70-80% of the market. Sixth and seventh approaches are unique to most of the developing countries. These seven approaches document seven business communication models. These models need different communication strategies to tap this market.

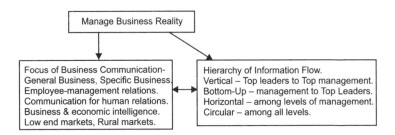

Fig. 7.2. Business Communication Model

Market Information Flow

Market information System (MIS) is organized flow of information among external and internal links. The concept is that the flow of the information is continuing, interactive with people and procedures to take market decisions.

Inflow and outflow of information and its sharing is important for successful business development viz marketing of the products, services and ideas. Outflow and inflow of information occur with ten major external links with the

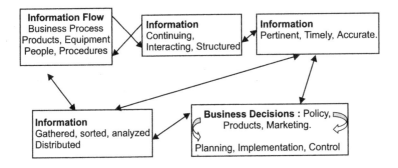

Fig. 7.3. Market Information Flow

corporate within the framework of national and international economies. Six external links: supply chain, distributors, whole-sellers and retailers, consumers, business competitors facilitate business development and market decisions about product and services. The two-way communications from other four external links of community, media, government and civic bodies regulate the business development with checks and balances and social responsibility.

Communication, strategic interactions and coordination, coherence (precision), persuasion, reinforcement are functions of external corporate communication links. These occur through different hierarchy of information needs of several business vendors. The mapping of information inflow and outflow between the business and external links, and its various focuses highlights the communication in business practices.

Within the business organization there will be several functions, some of which will be customers and suppliers to each other. Therefore, in a realistic business organization one will have a multitude of customer-supplier relationships of which many will be internal and many external. It is the dynamic between all the individual elements that will influence how communication channels are developed and proceed in this complex system.

Business Communications in a corporate can be focused from two perspectives: One, customer-supply chain relationships including both external and internal links; and two, employee-management relationship including internal links only. The dynamics of business communications are customer-supplier relationships in the context of product, services and people. The dynamics of business communications in employee-management relationship are in the context of performance, productivity and human relations.

Business communication tools

Business enterprise has three basic functions — Innovations, Marketing and Communications. The various business practices relate to these three functions.

Thus in any business enterprise marketing and communications are the two major tools for innovations of products and services. Innovations, Product life cycle management, marketing, and communication strategies are discussed in this context.

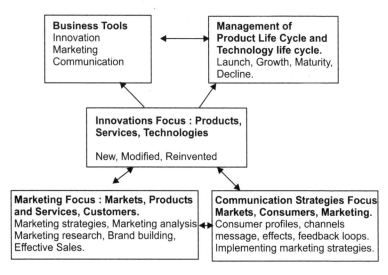

Fig. 7.4. Business Communication Tools

The Product Life Cycle refers to the succession of stages a product goes through. Product Life Cycle Management is the succession of strategies used by management as a product goes through its life cycle.

After a period of development product is introduced or launched into the market; it gains more and more customers as it grows; eventually the market stabilizes and the product becomes mature; then after a period of time the product is overtaken by development and the introduction of superior competitors, it goes into decline and is eventually withdrawn. However, most products fail in the introduction phase. Others have very cyclical maturity phases where declines see the product promoted to regain customers. Marketers' marketing mix strategies change as their products go through their life cycles. Advertising, for example, is informative in the introduction stage, persuasive in the growth and maturity stages, and is reminder-oriented in the decline stage.

Innovation is development of new product. It may be modifications of the old. This kind of new product is developed in response to customers' demands for better and with added utility; and to meet some of their immediate and urgent needs. The innovative as well re-innovative products are driven by consumer needs and may be the result of research and development.

Marketing in business is about products, customers and markets. In short, how business products and services reach the customers through markets and how customers in market segments access products and services of a business. The basic tools of marketing are: marketing strategies, market research and market analysis, pricing policies, supply chain, customer/consumer services and customer/consumer relations. These are intertwined and interdependent in its reach and functioning. The business practices of marketing products and services and ideas focus primarily on marketing strategies.

Market analysis and market research are the two major supporting tools of marketing strategies and communication is the essential component in market analysis and market research. We need both marketing strategies and communication strategies for marketing products and services, building brands and brand values, targeting segmented markets and targeted audiences and Sales for profitability. All marketing strategies not only need support from communication strategies but rather these play important roles in execution of market strategies at all the four stages.

Communication strategies (CS) are planned to implement marketing strategies. The focus of communication strategies is market and consumer. Therefore, the effort is to communicate about markets and consumers. This is two-way communication —from marketers to markets and consumers and from these two components to the marketers. Communication strategies are planned from five angles: characteristics, communication channels, message content, effects, and feedback loops.

Market characteristics such as geographic, regional, urban/ rural, high net/low mass are communicated to the marketers. Further, the characteristics of the segmented markets such as youth, old, women and children are communicated. The demographics and psychographics of the consumers in these markets are communicated. Marketers use this information and facts for market analysis in context of a particular products and services being considered. The product environment is in the market place, industries and business management offices.

Different communication channels are planned to reach different segments of markets according to reach and exposure in those segment markets. Rural market may have exposure through conventional TV and radio, outdoor publicity, billboards and interpersonal communications whereas the urban markets may have higher exposure to Internet, telephone and cinema etc. For effective communication, the channels are selected according to their high exposure for particular category of products and services, for specific segment markets — rural or urban, and according to the characteristics of the targeted consumers.

Message content is telling about the product verbally, through written word and through visual images. The message must project upfront what the product is, its enhanced qualities, how it satisfies the customer/consumer needs both overt and covert, price compatibility and affordability and the competitive products in the market. The message content contains persuasive appeals to buy. The message is further reinforced consistently through advertisements, product promotions, displays etc. In short, message must convey what the business wants to convey and its strength and credibility lies in the final act of sale.

Businesses and customers/consumers are both sender and receivers according to the message situations since circular communication is necessary condition for viability and reinforcement of the messages both from the marketers and consumers. This suggest the feedback loops from senders to receivers and from intervening market elements for better understanding of consumer demands and satisfaction and at the same time what marketers want to convey about the products and services.

There are channel noises. This could be customers/consumers satisfaction or dissatisfaction conveyed about the products, customer services and customer relations. There may be complaints about channels usage and credibility. It is important to take care of channel noises.

The business marketer is concerned about both short term and long term effects of product messages in terms of buying behavior of customers and consumers, their attitudes towards products and services, particular brands, and image of the company in general. Marketer is also concerned, and it is of interest to him also to assess the change in those attitudes overtime and factors responsible for it. These are some of the short-term effects. These are assessed in terms of demands for the products.

The long terms effects are assessed when there is actual purchase of the product and when services sold are used not once but again and again. Quite likely, the products and services may be rejected either initially or after initial use. These long-term effects are assessed in sales of the products and profitability of the products and markets.

The effects are assessed by feedback loops from the customers and consumers to the marketer and back. 'Effects' is essential component in all the four stages of marketing strategies. On one hand, these several feedback loops feed about the positive and negative effects of the products and markets differently at all the four stages, and on the other hand these feedback loops create better understanding about the products, its visibility, attitudes and buying behavior.

Effects are assessed by marketers through market analysis and market research. The effects are conveyed to the marketing associated management levels and top-management for action through interpersonal and interface communications supported by technological databases etc.

8

Communication Research Models

Communication research focuses on local, regional, national and international issues from communication point. The early researches and confrontation with new communication situations stimulated further communication research in specific areas of source, audience, message, channels and effects (both mass media and interpersonal), communication rules, content and contextual research. Besides this, urban, urban periphery and rural areas are also researched for the specific related issues.

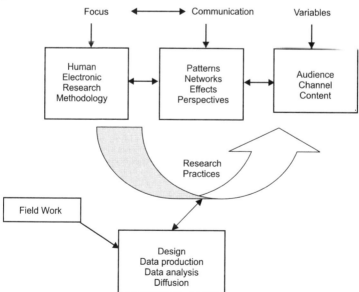

Fig. 8.1. Communication Research Variables

Thus the research models differ according to the above focuses, and categorizations and they are issue related. Even the research models are impacted by the upcoming and newer applications of media technologies. Research in different communication variables changes the communication scenario over a time period. Such changing communication scenario can represent specific research models. Thus there could be numerous research models. To present them from every single perspective would be beyond the scope of this book. We present only salient communication research models.

Research is conducted with greater sensitivity to cultural and political concerns and with methods reflecting those concerns. New Research methodologies, new research techniques are experimented and adopted to gain better insights in human communications.

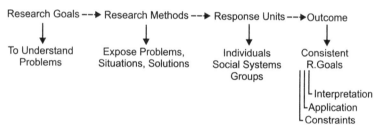

Fig. 8.2. Social Research Investigative Paradigm-1

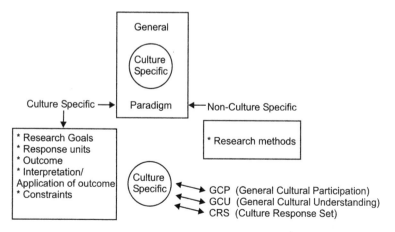

Fig. 8.3. Social Research Investigative Paradigm-2

The research practices are constrained by practical problems and some of those problems are politics and culture specific.

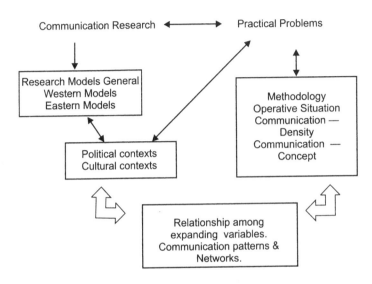

Fig. 8.4. Practical Constraints in Communication Research

Over a period of time different Mass Communication Models developed in consequence to our changing understanding of the concepts, elements of communication process, and communication rules. Communication research facilitated these.

9

Models for Communication Planning and Strategies

Communication strategies are based on field experiences and theoretical analysis of focused activity areas. Varied communication strategies are used (planned) both by government and people to communicate effectively to their targeted audience. Communication planning involves — communication strategies, media planning (channel planning) and resource management culminating in communication policies.

The dimensions focused in the strategies must be managed well in order to make the programs delivered to the targeted audience effectively.

Fig. 9.1. Communication Planning and Policies

The interaction of State, market and public is significant for communication planning.

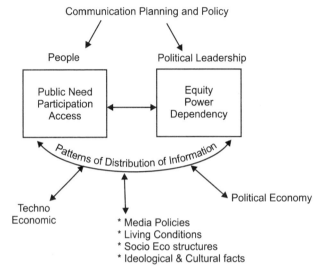

Fig. 9.2. **Political Economy of Communication Planning**

Different components of vertical, horizontal and cyclical communication planning structure the policies.

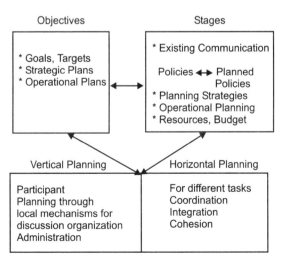

Fig. 9.3. **Components of Communication Planning**

The planning constraints could be human, technical and other resources.

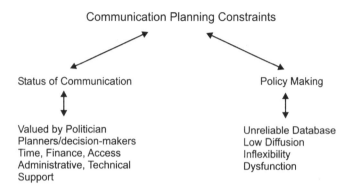

Fig. 9.4. Communication Planning Constraints

These strategies could be both positive and negative. They are both media and interpersonal focused. Nature, forms and types of communication strategies suggest mostly who would use these strategies, with what objectives and with what effects.

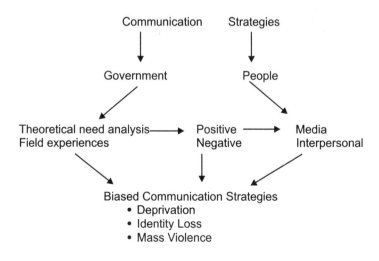

Fig. 9.5. Communication Strategies Model 1

The assumption is that biased communication strategies create deprivation, loss of identities and mass violence.

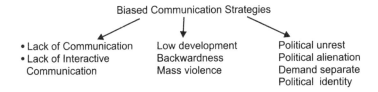

Fig. 9.6. Communication Strategies Model 2

National governments use, manipulate and control media technologies to channel their own viewpoints and policies and to set political and social agenda for people's thinking. People use power of media to express their demands, viewpoints and set their own agenda. This public agenda sets the government for interaction with the public's viewpoints and opens way for public discourses on many issues.

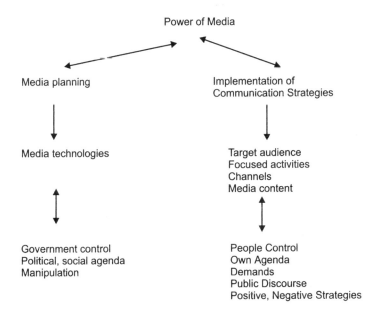

Fig. 9.7. Power of Media Control

The International governments, organizations and communities control and influence the media to set political agenda with the national governments and social agenda for people. Media in combination with information, education, communication and motivation (IECM) strategies control and influence the communities.

Media control is a vertical strategy. Mass media can be the ideological army in support of globalization, but can also become the grassroots weapons to fight its impact. Ethics in Media is challenging.

Epilogue

The dynamic interplay of source, message, communication channels and audience is necessary for effective and successful communication. Such communication has concerns for its priorities and functions. Priorities differ from developed to developing countries. Communication functions differ and get prioritized according to the priorities set by the countries and consumption of communication channels that are socially constructed and maintained practices.

The changing communication scenario globally, creates demands and priorities for communication conceptualizations and its diverse perspectives. The functions, applications and practice of communications also keep changing. The changing communication scenario presents diverse communication models. Some of these developed on the earlier foundation models and suggested new, useful and significant concepts, which were later developed; and others present new dimensions.

International development theorists and practitioners have conceptualized development from various perspectives such as social change, modernization, progress and alternations in life styles. All the perspectives have encompassed 'growth', the economic growth viz industrialization, agrarian, and technological growth and the social growth identified with structural and value changes.

Development in developing countries vis-à-vis providing quality of life to people through modernization has been one of the major concerns of western countries since 50's. An historical analysis of development models since 50s provides insight into the changing development models. These changed with the changing dynamics of development, and the technological breakthrough in the mass media channels.

There have been four approaches to understand underdevelopment and how to do development. These are: modernization through dominant paradigm, Interdependency model, Basic needs model and Communication for Development Model in national and international contexts. These approaches are exemplars of development and development communication.

There is a change, and since 70s the national governments and the people themselves for their own societies have conceived the development. All later models are country specific. The last six decades of research has revealed that role of communication in development is significant and it has changed with the change in development models.

Development Communication scenario has changed globally in the last six decades. There have been four-pronged major changes. The focus of development has changed, nature of development demands and issues have changed, new communication channels are available and the characteristics of the audience have changed.

In 80s, the role of Development Communication changed over to the dynamic process of bringing development to the people for whom development is envisaged. It is conceptualized as information, education, communication within cultural matrix and motivation for participation in development (IECM). The varied development communication approaches facilitate actions for evolving effective communication strategy for development projects.

New conceptual and practical demands on development and communications suggest reengineering and reinvention. Development innovations, civil engagement, enabling environment, social accountability and participation, civil society in communication driven development, and self-regulation of civil society in development and e-government are some of the important factors in the restructured development scenario of current 2000 decade. This calls for mainstreaming e-development to shape our lives differently.

Globalization is the major focus of international communication in this era. The process of globalization is the basic context in international communication.globalization is being approached from diverse perspectives of political, economics and trade migration, infotainment and communication. Globalization occurs in social political, economic, cultural, information society, and media contexts. International Communication processes work through mass media and interpersonal communication channels focusing at these contexts of world community.

The interaction of various world communities, exposure to world mass media and communication are the key factors to International Communication theories, strategies, and practice. International Communication has five major focuses: conflict resolution and peace processes, development of developing countries, technological and economic challenges and visions that the international communication through information age and knowledge economy has created, and intercultural and cross-cultural communications within the international framework.

The major Paradigm of 2000 decade is Technology Paradigm. IT is becoming an important factor in the new growth theory beside labor and capital. Information communication technologies (ICT) are important. They have been both evolutionary and revolutionary, giving connectivity both in personal and professional life of people. The present scenario is that all technologies are integrated and converged and that provides holistic information connectivity. The social and economic repercussions of the advances in ICT are so great that the term "information revolution" is probably justifiable. The new ICT model has made many old paradigms and theories of communication obsolete. The update model is technology networking and technology convergence.

Technological advancements vis-à-vis development of new media technologies created six Communication Revolutions:

in Writing, Printing, Broadcasting, Films, Telecommunications, Computer and e-technologies, and Quantum computing, nanotechnology and fuel cell technology of 2000 decade,(the last one yet to be revolutionized). These technologies introduced at different decades of the centuries revolutionized communication because of advancement in technologies over a period of time; and that expanded their different functional forms and supporting-ethnotronic technologies. It further changed their program contents and functions tuning to the audience demand.

The six Communication Revolutions since early 8th through14th century to date have exploded in information revolution and created new perspectives for media technologies, contexts and impacts through changing media technologies over time. Technological changes brought different issues on the forefront. These communication revolutions focused on giving better connectivity to human beings through both machines and humans.

The explosive growth of the World Wide Web through Internet in 90s, its burst in late 90s, obscured the rapid progression of the Internet. But the current build-out in 2000 decade marked by a proliferation of mobile Internet devices, the spread of Internet protocol telephony, and the emergence of spin-off technologies will refocus attention on the Internet

Communications revolutions over the centuries created more and more of industrial products, consumer products and cultural products to develop and improve the living conditions around the world. Computer has become an integrated technology for other technologies to usher. Without it many of the newer technology applications, devices, and innovations will be handicapped.

There is impact of ICT in practice on the media scene, the network society, digital-divide, health improvement, economic growth and poverty reduction, empowerment of women, and in achieving millennium development goals.

Such techno-social revolution would need a dynamic set of IT entrepreneurs, business leaders, highly placed government officials, international donors, social entrepreneurs and leading academicians. In collaboration and coordination with one another this 'network' will find trigger points where IT can become a catalyst for development and shape public policy related to IT.

The fourth, fifth and the sixth communication revolutions have been the harbinger of convergent technologies suggesting that different upcoming technologies of computer, telecommunication, laser, quantum, fuel cell technology and nanotechnologies; all have to work in unison and are interdependent on one another to develop myriad applications.

Social equity and public policy challenges of transformative technology are being faced by developing countries — understanding the social and public policy dimensions. The focus is how social equity and the human condition is being affected by the emerging technologies (both ICT and other technologies) as well as what mechanisms and learning processes are in place or have been developed to be in place to assist government and public stakeholders groups engaged in the decision making processes associated with these new technologies.

The intercultural communication models addresses the significance of images — self-image, other-image and inter-cultural image expressed through our cultural resources both tangible and intangible.

In context to this framework the focus is on cultural identity, multiculturalism, cultural experiences and influences, and the cultural diversity. These variables create dilemmas and tensions. Cultures make efforts to achieve intercultural communication effectiveness despite these limitations. Therefore, the model for intercultural communication effectiveness is to develop functional communication styles that allow us to develop positive relationships so necessary for adaptation to the alien culture.

Communication among people across nations, countries, and cultures is important. Since from all perspectives, it involves communicating with diverse cultures and understanding of those cultures, and therefore focusing on social phenomena. Thus social theory of national identity becomes significant.

The outcome of interaction of various cultural resources may be amalgamation, integration, adaptation and negotiation of certain cultural resources. In such interactions, communication is a dynamic process whereby verbal and nonverbal human behavior is perceived and responded to.

There is a pragmatic interest in intercultural communication as cultures must be known and understood in the right communication perspective for wider political, social, educational, commercial, and technological ramifications. The dynamics of intercultural communication are building intercultural climate, social perceptions and intercultural variance.

In intercultural interaction, vis-à-vis cultural diversity, in any cultural environment, unless the differences we represent are appreciated and valued, those differences will tend to hinder rather than help the performance. Therefore, to mange diversity well whether in a social set up, or in work place; it is necessary to recognize, value, respect, and utilize differences to the benefit of the host cultural institutions. Our differences represent the greatest value as well as the greatest threat. At international level in immigrant societies like USA, the Melting Pot Model, Transcultural Model, Mosaic Model and Media Exposure Model may create integration in cultural diversity.

The development practitioners learnt from the experiences that culture specific models are necessary for successful development; since every culture's development demands are unique in tune with its material and non-material cultural resources. Many times, threat to cultural identity may block some development programs.

The impact of Information technologies does facilitate intercultural communication but they can also create cultural dilemmas and tensions by exposing people to multicultural and global perspectives.

Communication is an important component in every human activity. It is effective when it is managed well. Therefore, it is important how communication is managed in various streams for effective delivery of ideas, products, and services. The management could be of both human and non-human communications (computer, telecommunication etc). It is an expertise area. *The focus of management of human communication is essentially the five dimensions: creating awareness, disseminating information, delivery of services, ideas and products, coordinating linkages for both human and non-human communications and better administration of campaigns, services and linkages. Communication competence is significant to manage these five dimensions.*

Management focus is addressed to health care, intercultural communications, development communications, information and communications technologies, business communications and managing knowledge economies, conflict management and knowledge management.

Business communication models suggest that Business Communications in a corporate can be focused from three perspectives: One, customer-supply chain relationships including both external and internal links; two, employee-management relationship including internal links only; and three consumer-product relationship. The dynamics of business communications are customer-supplier relationships in the context of product, services and people. The dynamics of business communications in employee-management relationship are in the context of performance, productivity and human relations. The consumer-product relationship is in the context of product markets and marketing strategies, and consumer behavior.

The strength of internal business communication lies in coordinating the three core processes of people, strategies and operations and motivating for Action implementation. Implementation is in a way exposing reality and acting on it. Interpersonal communication dynamics play significant role in this context. Feedback is important component in the interpersonal interaction process. There is technology support to interpersonal communication also.

Employee and Management Interaction focus on building and upgrading the capabilities of the organization and its employees, surfacing the business reality, and communication about business strategy. This calls for robust and candid dialogue strategies.

The Communication Patterns in business can be top-down, bottom to top, bottom-bottom, and circular. The communication patterns with customers in the supply chain can be two-ways, circular and with many feedback loops. Communication mode is interpersonal — both formal and informal, both in groups and one-on-one and supported by technologies. The communication patterns with consumers of goods and services are both formal and informal interpersonal communication modes and various media channels.

Scope of business communication lies in three domains: B2B – business to business, B2C business to customer, and C2C customer to customer. These three have different business as well communication focuses. The three business communication approaches deal with specific relationships associated with these.

The four business concepts: know the market forces and recognize the changing market dynamics, business leaders must do the right things right, confront the reality, and accepted set of values present the business communication perspective that can impede or facilitate company leaders to recognize the changing market dynamics and the business communication tools.

The various Business Communication Models take seven approaches: general and specific business approach, communications for employee–management relationships, for human relations in businesses, business communication to rural markets and to the poor having low level purchasing capability, communicating through economic intelligence analysis, and economics of business communications.

Business Communication Practices focus on three basic functions — Innovations, Marketing and Communications. Marketing and communications are the two major tools for innovations (products and services). Product life cycle suggests strategies for the differing stages of the PLC, and technology life cycle. We need both marketing strategies and communication strategies for marketing products and services, building brands and brand values, targeting segmented markets and targeted audiences and Sales for profitability.

Business organization functions in dynamic environment of marketing. And nothing can be more dynamic than changing consumer profiles, attitudes and behavior. Thus the core of marketing is identifying and understanding the customers. And critical to this intelligence is the ability to update the information in tune with the dynamism of the market environment

The business practices of marketing products and services and ideas focus primarily on marketing strategies. Communication strategies (CS) are planned to implement marketing strategies. Communication strategies are planned from five angles: characteristics, communication channels, message content, effects, and feedback loops. All marketing strategies not only need support from Communication strategies but rather CS play important role in execution of market strategies at all the four stages. Market analysis and market research are the two major supporting tools of marketing strategies and communication is the essential component in market analysis and market research.

The urgent challenges faced by managers today in global businesses could be high levels of business complexity and rapid change. There are high demands for leadership attitudes and skills throughout the business to analyze issues, execute strategies, and drive for results. The key ingredient for globalization in business is strategic partnership with the local player and offering high level of service quality. The communication channels and modes, communication partners and focuses have changed with the global economic order undergoing constant change and facing new challenges like outsourcing, foreign investments both in financial markets and infrastructures, and exports

The multiple channels of national and international media play triple role of acting as information and knowledge broker, and facilitator for the public, businesses and government. National media sets agenda for business through public, businesses and government. International media channels facilitate globalization of businesses by creating global visibility of the consumers, products and services and markets.

Research has been a significant and essential component in developing the Communication discipline. Both empirical and theoretical researches have helped in ironing out the wrinkles as well developing more insights, new dimensions and components in the discipline.

Communication research methodology has evolved and developed overtime with the changing communication priorities, functions, audience demographics, media consumption, advancement in ICT and the need and significance of supporting role of both interpersonal communication and media channels. Communication research has facilitated these changes. The practical problems in communication research have impeded as well stimulated more research. Researches also advocated, supported and developed different perspectives from which communication has been studied and applied overtime

Communication planning, policy and strategies are important for effective communication. Role of development strategist, vision of political leaders, administrators and functionaries is significant in this context. The positive and negative participation of people is not an ignored factor but equally significant.

Communication planning both long range and short range is efficient and equitable use of communication resources for the realization of communication policies. It identifies the priorities, possibilities and pressures. We do face communication-planning constraints such as the conceptual framework of communication in a particular society, political will and the vision of its leaders. Further, the status constraints could be time, finance, administrative and technical support and access

Practice of communication planning is differentiated into

horizontal and vertical planning. Horizontal planning is coordination, integration and cohesion of the different tasks of planning. Vertical planning is through participation.

Communication policies are sets of principles and norms established to guide the behavior of the communication systems. Their orientation is fundamental and long range although they may have operational implications of short-range significance. They are shaped in the context of society's general approach to communication. Policy making criteria, strategic planning and communication strategies are important in this context.

Communication strategies are based on field experiences and theoretical analysis of focused activity areas. The nature, forms and types of communication strategies are planned accordingly. Some of these are planned others are unplanned and spontaneous. These communication strategies could be positive, negative and mixed i.e. used both as positive and negative strategies according to the situations. These strategies control communications.

The Future

The change may occur due to changes in modalities of communications, both people oriented and technology oriented. New communication technologies may come up. Along with this, newer needs and demands may turn up. Social attitudes and values may change for newer needs and demands. People become more aware, educated and motivated in these diverse contexts and setup new modalities for both interpersonal and media communication. In order to present and explain the widened scope of different communication perspectives; more and advanced level Communication Models will evolve. Therefore, over the coming decades we look forward to more and more of advance level Models supporting the changing and newer perspectives from which communications may be studied, analyzed, applied, and practiced. The academicians and practitioners in communication discipline would be looking for innovative approaches.